WHATDADDY
DIDN'T KNOW

LETTERS OF A FATHERLESS CHILD

LANCE BRAZELTON

For permission requests, write to the author at brazelton100@gmail.com

Edited by: Marcia Burnette, Tamia Hampton, Victoria Knight, Doug Martinson

Cover Design: Barbara Upshaw – Aura Graphics and Design

Illustrations: Lance Brazelton

Published by: Lance Brazelton

Library of Congress Control Number: 2016902841

ISBN-13: 978-0-692-64401-0

ISBN-10: 0-692-64401-6

CONTENTS

Dedication

This book is dedicated to the women who nurtured me, supported my dreams, and gave me endless amounts of love.

Johanna S. Brazelton

Mozell E. Brazelton

Vickie L. Brazelton

Praise for Lance

By Brenda Darcel Harris-Lee

When I met the young Lance Brazelton I was immediately struck by his mature demeanor, his politeness and his ability to completely focus on every word you were saying, making you feel that you were the only person in the room. "This young man," I thought to myself …"this young is going places – he is going to contribute something important to this world one day." Well, that day is here and Lance's book, "What Daddy Didn't Know – The Letters of a Fatherless Child" is a book like no other. Lance Brazelton has creatively harnessed his hurt, his devastating pain, his pinnacles of joy, his self-made success, his utter loneliness, his deep sense of community, his most private inner thoughts, and truly…his absolute soul. Lance has not only captured all of these emotions and more, but he has managed to pour all of it onto the pages of a book so mesmerizing, so complex and captivating, that I defy anyone to pick it up and put it without weeping, laughing and shouting in triumph for this young man who knows, without a doubt, how to walk through life with purpose and with understanding. Lance has done all of this while defying adverse circumstances and rising above that which could have destroyed him. "What Daddy Didn't Know" will help every child without a father find their worth and seek their destiny; it will steer every single parent to realize the importance of showering their children with love and building in them an innate sense of self-worth and self-esteem; and ultimately, this book will change the national conversation and redirect the paradigm around fatherless children, their potential, their contributions, and their impact on our world now and in the future.

Brenda Darcel Harris-Lee

Founder – CEO, International Black Health Alliance

Foreword

By David Person

We parents have our cherished memories of moments in our children's lives. But our children have their own stories, their own recollections of their formative years.

Some of those memories expose the weaknesses and failures of the adults in their lives. Some of them reflect the immaturity and uncertainty of youth.

In What Daddy Didn't Know, Lance Brazelton does a great job of telling his story, taking readers inside the challenges of growing up in poverty as the oldest child of a single mother. Lance is brutally transparent. He shares his fears, tears and disappointments. He confesses troubling mistakes. And in radical defiance of macho stereotypes, Lance proudly professes his love for his girlfriends while also being open about his uncertainties and questions about the love he shares with them.

But What Daddy Didn't Know also is a love letter to Lance's absentee father. The young man openly yearns for him, sharing the daily details of his life while also asking him many of the questions that boys ask their fathers. Lance also questions his father's absence, openly wrestling with the impact and meaning of not having the man in his life.

Amazingly, Lance is never bitter. Arguably, he has every right to be. But the tone of this book, despite the challenges this young man has to face – missteps by some of the adults in his life, the death of key family members, near brushes with the law, his discovery of love and sex, the temptations of the streets – is overwhelmingly, relentlessly positive.

What Daddy Didn't Know is a revelation of Lance Brazelton's heart. He discloses a sensitivity that many young men would be reluctant to share.

In truth, this book is not a literary masterpiece. The prose and poetry can be a bit rugged. But this book doesn't need to be a literary classic. It is an emotional one.

Those who read it will get a great sense of the ambitions, fears, optimism and despair that inhabit the hearts and minds of many young black men. And hopefully, it will put a human face on these young brothers who far too often are relegated to being social ills and statistics.

Lance Brazelton is neither. He's more than the circumstances in which he was raised. He's a living, breathing young man full of faith and hope.

Readers soon will know this. And hopefully one day, his father will know it too. Wherever he is.

David Person

Member of USA Today Board of Contributors, and Social Justice Activist, and writer for Message Magazine and the Ministry Matters website.

Introduction

My name is Lance Christopher Brazelton, and I'm twenty one-years-old. I'm an author, publisher, poet, producer, illustrator, and music artist.

As a young boy growing up without my father in my life, I was inspired to write this book because I was determined to not become a statistic of fatherless children. There are millions of fatherless children around the world, but who is discussing the tragedy of this topic? How many people really know the true story behind every fatherless child?

My intended audience for this book includes fatherless children (boys/girls), single parents, and soon to be fathers.

I wrote this book in an attempt to touch the hearts of everyone who was once lost, confused, and clueless of their purpose in life. What Daddy Didn't Know reveals the thought process of fatherless children, and how decisions are most important in your adolescent years.

I wanted to show other kids like me that with their Heavenly Fathers guidance, they can turn their lives into some of the most inspirational stories to ever be told.

This is my childhood told through letters and poems to my absentee father. Everything I've experienced, witnessed, and overcame, is something my biological father never knew; but it's also something my Heavenly Father gave me the strength to endure.

WHatDaddy
DIDN'T KNOW

Chapter 1
"Mama's First Bloomed"

"Mama's First Bloomed"

I was Mother's first born who was sent from up above,

And even when she hates the things I do, she still shows me love.

Can't nobody fly higher than this beautiful dove!

And can't nobody replace the very first face I saw in my life.

I never needed a calculator because I could always count on my mother,

But when it came to my dad it seemed like everything was a blur.

I was born into sin, so please excuse my set of horns,

And remember that every rose has its set of thorns.

They separated a rose from its roots when they cut my umbilical cord,

But still I grew in the protection of Christ; Jesus is my shield and sword.

You promised to take care of me, and in the future I promise to take care of you,

O mama, how It's a blessing to be born from you.

Together we bloomed.

Lance Brazelton

Mama's First Bloomed

November 10, 1994

Dear Dad,

Hey Dad! Today was the day I was born, but I was surprised to not see you in the room when I came out of Mother's womb. She had me at Huntsville Hospital in some State named Alabama, wherever that is. I was so excited to finally match the faces with the voices that would talk to me, for they would keep me company while I was still developing. I hope that Mother continues to tell me bedtime stories even though I'm no longer in her tummy. Everyone was so excited to see me and wouldn't keep their filthy paws off of me. Birth is a hard process not only for the mother, but the child as well. All I ask is don't wake me up every time a family member comes into the room, or else I'll have a gift in my diaper for them to unwrap. It's nice for family members to stop by, but their presence isn't an alarm clock so let me sleep in. I remember every single night Mother would read me bedtime stories from this book called The Bible. I remember Psalms 51: 5 said, "Behold, I was shaped in iniquity; and in sin did my mother conceive me." I was told ahead of time that I would be born into sin, so does this make me a bad person? I didn't ask to be born into sin, nor did I ask to be born at all! I was planted and forced to grow in sins dark soil. Please just forgive me and excuse my set of horns, for I pray that they'll dissolve away one day. When one of my cousins came into the room, she automatically scooped me up like a ground ball and covered me in her kisses. I cannot seem to ever understand what my cousin was talking about though. I'm supposed to learn the English language, so please don't talk to me with that "goo goo ga ga" crap; either you pronounce it right or don't say it at all. Later on that night I got hungry, so I decided to start screaming so they would feed me. My shrilling cry was like the bell that grandma rings outside when its dinner time and all the kids run inside to eat. I got fed every time I did it, so I used it to my advantage. When I'm drinking my milk, I'm like an alcoholic at the bar; bottoms up till it's gone then refill the bottle up! I love being a kid because the only responsibility I have is to eat whenever I want; it's like a buffet I don't have to pay for. Mother bought me my first teddy bear from the gift shop; it was turquoise blue, yellow, and white. It was hard trying to think of a name for something when you have a freshly built brain. I always had to boo boo, so I just named him Boo Boo Bear. I slept with him every single night, but I would still prefer to sleep in Mother's arms over anything. The safest place in the world is inside Mother's arms. She's a strong woman if she was able to push my big head out! I know for sure that I'm safe in the barriers of her arms, because she wouldn't let me go even if the moon turned red. She tells me stories about my great grandmother all the time; her name was Mamuka. Mother says she would be happy to see me. I would think to myself that if she wanted to see me, then why wouldn't she just come by the hospital like everyone else? I never could understand, but I know I'll see her one day; maybe she'll come by the house when I'm released to go home for the first time. Dad, it's a wonder of the world why I didn't see you the day I was born, but it's alright because I know I'll see you soon, and you'll be there to see me take my first steps on my chubby little legs. I promise I'll bloom into everything you want me to be and more. I know there's a reason for why I was born today.

Not from Lance, but from the Heart of his Soul,

Your Child,

Lance

Chapter 2
"Father Where Art Thou"

"Father Where Art Thou"

Will I ever see my big brother from another mother?

Every day I kiss my little sister from another mister.

I vision portraits of memories that could've been painted by you
and me,

And every thought born in my mind reminds me of you.

I feel like I'm behind bars, and I'm only a child now,

I want to express myself to you, but I just can't express how.

I'm living life on the edges while dodging the dark presage,

Please come back like the pigeon and don't stay like the message.

I miss you.

Father Where Art Thou

June 15, 1997

Dear Dad,

Hey Dad, it's me, Lance. Today was Father's Day, and we made cards at Summer Camp to honor our fathers. I brought mine home, but there was no father to give it to. Father, where art thou? Ever since I've come into this world, I haven't seen your face, nor a sign that you still exist. I overhear conversations that Mother has with the family, and I hear them say I look just like you, Dad. I've never seen you before, so is that a good thing or a bad thing? What do you look like period? Do you think about me at all, and do we share the same emotions? I never had the chance to crawl in your direction, so am I supposed to follow in your footsteps now that I can walk? I've seen some footprints outside the door, but they lead down a road so dark that I can't see what's in the distance. Are those the footsteps that you left for me to follow? Or is that the road you forbid me to travel? I'll never know the answers to my questions if there's no instructor to teach me. I guess I might be on my own. My messages are more than just letters, for they're words written from my heart to whom they may concern. I'm concerned about many things, like if you're going to return one day, or if I'm wasting time waiting for you when I'm supposed to be following in your footsteps.... Are you waiting on me somewhere out there in the world? Mother told me how excited the family was when I took my first steps in the living room. She said I became trouble on the move after I started walking. It seems like you have to master one thing in order to learn things related to it, like how I had to learn to crawl before I could learn to walk. I have a little sister now; her name's Jada. She was born this year on January 29th. Of course we don't have the same father if I'm writing a letter to you about it, or do we? Mother also told me that I have an older brother on your side of the family, but how will I know if I'm walking by him every day or not? What does he look like? Do we favor each other, and are we close to the same age? And do all three of us share the same blood? There are many answers hidden from my questions. I go outside to play every day, and I always wonder if I'll walk into you the same day I step off the front porch on my own. Maybe one day I'll follow your footsteps that disappear into the darkness in the distance. Is that where I'll finally find you? And why is it dark in your direction? When Mother stands with me at the bus stop I look down the road and wonder if I'll see you walking towards us, but every time it's just the same old drunken fiend stumbling through the neighborhood. Mother tells me to stay away from people like that who can't control their mind. Dad, I wonder why you left me without letting me know where I could find you? I collect questions in my mind, and then I search the vast world for answers. You left nothing but footsteps that lead down a dark road, and I don't know if I'm supposed to follow your tracks, nor do I know if you'll ever return; I can only wonder.

Not from Lance, but from the Heart of his Soul,

Your Child,

Lance

Chapter 3
"Little Footprints by the Grave"

"Little Footprints by the Grave"

Roses red as blood; Violets blue as the sky,

Life is a beautiful blessing and Jesus said so am I.

GOD sent me from Heaven, and I don't know the reason,

So I try to learn something new when the world substitutes
seasons.

Every day's not going to be sunny; I can hear a dark cloud
around the way,

But if Mother looks into my eyes then she'll know that
everything's okay.

She said I was by her side when I didn't have to be there,

Now the graveyard knows what size shoes I wear.

We recited a prayer and stamped it with a kiss,

Then she held me and said ignorance is truly bliss.

Father can you tell me what my Mother's words mean?

Lance Brazelton

Little Footprints by the Grave

March 18, 2000

Dear Dad,

Hey Dad, I had a weird day today. My granddaddy died, whatever that means.... Mother told me that he turned into an angel. If I were an angel, I would fly away to watch the world from up high in the sky. We got dressed up and went to church to see him. When we got there I saw him sleeping in a glossy-looking box at the front of the church. We walked in a single-file line just like in school, but no one tried to wake him up. I couldn't understand why everyone was crying, but before I knew it I felt a drop of water roll down my right cheek. I was crying and I didn't even know why, I guess tears are just contagious.... I wiped the tears off my face with the tip of my tie, and I asked Mother why everyone was crying? She told me that they were just sad; so I asked why they were sad if he was just sleeping? I thought about going to the front of the church and waking him up so everyone could stop crying like a bunch of babies. That's when Mother told me that he wasn't going to wake up. I asked why, and she said because he had already woken up in a place called Heaven. I remember Mother telling me about Heaven once before, but I never really understood how you could get there. I asked Mother, and she told me that the only way to get there is by flapping your set of wings if you earned them here on earth. After the pastor said a couple of words about my granddaddy, they started to migrate outside to a field behind the church. When we walked out there I saw a bunch of cool shaped rocks, and all of them had names written on them. It was strange because I could feel every letter on the rocks. The pastor read a couple of lines out the Bible, and they lowered my granddaddy's glossy box down into the ground. How would he get back out once he comes back from visiting Heaven? I asked Mother the same question, and she told me that he wasn't ever going to come back, for he'll be waiting for us at the pearly gates. I didn't even know Heaven was surrounded by gates; it must be an amazing place to live. I hope I have a reserved room for when I move there; then maybe my granddaddy would come by and visit my room every day. I pray that I have a pair of angel wings hung up like a leather jacket, waiting to be placed on my back.

I asked Mother if she knew where you were, and she told me a story that confused my mind. She said that you were in jail from being involved in a robbery. I wondered if anyone got harmed during the robbery, or if you were even guilty for it at all. She also told me that jail wasn't a place that I would want to go, so why is it that you went there? Is there something special there that Mother doesn't know about? Or do you have something to bring me from this place called jail? Are you already out and on your way back home as I'm writing this letter? I never hear anything from you, so did you forget about me??? I'm pretty sure that you'll have a good explanation for why you went to jail. I'm not sure if I'm supposed to follow in your footsteps from what Mother told me about jail. It sounds like a dark and scary place, and the sound of it sends chills up my spine. Maybe one day those chills will turn into your hands holding me as you tuck me in at night.

Not from Lance, but from the Heart of his Soul,

Your Child,

Lance

Chapter 4
"The Christ in Christmas"

"The Christ in Christmas"

Santa Clause never delivered the desires on my wish list,

Because it's Jesus who puts the Christ in Christmas.

Auntie Lene I don't know what I would do without you,

I want to say thank you for my gifts, and for the knowledge of the truth.

I know a thank you between me and you goes without saying.

Everyday I'm praying thanking the Lord for a spirit like you.

Till the seas go dry, till my soul flies high,

I will forever appreciate the things that you do.

Earth is colder than Pluto; so what's real love?

I remain comfortable inside the warmth of your hugs.

I know you'll get your thanks in Heaven, for you're a beautiful bloomed blessing;

But before that journey begins I wanted to say thank you once again.

The Christ in Christmas

December 25, 2001

Dear Dad,

Hey Dad, I thought that maybe you would be Santa Clause if I stayed up all night on Christmas Eve. We spent the holidays with my Grandma Mozell at my Auntie Lene's house. I saw my Auntie Lene putting gifts under the Christmas tree. I was quiet as a mouse as I stealthily snuck back into my room. I now have proof that Santa Clause isn't real, and he's never existed. Do you exist??? I sometimes get a warm feeling in my chest when I think about what will be said when I finally see you. When everyone woke up on Christmas the next morning, I could smell the scent of delicious food flying through the air. Man, I couldn't wait to get in there and start stuffing my face. I looked outside and saw a blanket of beautiful white snow on the ground. It usually doesn't snow on Christmas; it seemed to only happen in the Christmas movies on TV. My sister Jada and I did what any other kids would do, we went outside and played in the snow. We had a snowball fight, but we had to stop because Jada got smoked in the face with a snowball. After the snowball fight, we attempted to build a snowman, key word "attempted." We failed miserably; our snowman looked like a pile of old dog poop. We got mud in it while we were trying to roll the snow together; they make it look so easy on TV, but my life isn't a movie, right? My favorite part about Christmas is opening my gifts, and then trying out all of my new stuff. I look at all my gifts on Christmas Eve to see if you put a present under the tree to surprise me, but there was never a gift that said it was from Dad. I still got a lot of gifts from Mother, Grandma Mozell, and Auntie Lene. I hate it when someone gives me clothes instead of toys. I would be expecting a new video game, but when I open it, I see nothing but some socks. It started to make more sense as I got older; I've learned that Christmas isn't even about the gifts. Christmas is about celebrating the birth of Jesus. It's Jesus who puts the Christ in Christmas!

After I found out that Santa Clause wasn't real, I started to recognize the real true meaning of Christmas. My Auntie Lene buys everyone whatever is on their wish list; but she also told me that the materialistic stuff really doesn't matter. She told me that we are given a gift everyday when we wake up in the morning, and it's up to us to thank the Lord for allowing us to see another day. I thought Santa Clause would bring gifts on Christmas Eve, but I was wrong. Jesus brings me the gift of life every single morning. Every day is a celebration because Jesus is the one who puts the Christ in Christmas. When I found out the true meaning of Christmas, it made me wonder if Jesus slips gifts into our lives that we haven't noticed yet.... Have you noticed me yet? Sometimes I feel as though I'm invisible to you. Christ is invisible to me, but He's familiar to the touch; so I know I can reach you if I pray hard enough.

Not from Lance, but from the Heart of his Soul,

Your Child,

Lance

Chapter 5
"Childhood Trophies"

"Childhood Trophies"

New generation, we are the nation,

The man in the mirror is my inspiration.

My hands in the sky with my eyes on the prize,

You can tell I'm not playing by the look in my eyes.

In this life of hard knocks they're going to try and knock you,

And if you start to lose stick and move like a boxer.

Stand your ground and show no slack,

And if you fall down, rebound and bounce back.

I have a hero's heart, but a hooligan's what they see,

I pray that someone somewhere prays for me.

If you fail, please come back like you never hit your knees,

A quitter never wins, and a winner never quits;

What you struggle for is what you get.

Childhood Trophies

June 12, 2003

Dear Dad,

Hey Dad, guess who has the right to say that they're a champion.... Our All-Star baseball team went all the way to the finals, and we won the championship for our age group; I'm the one who dove and caught the winning out! I even have a trophy to prove my accomplishments on the grass diamond. I've always enjoyed playing sports while growing up. I love to come and play baseball at Phillips Park every Friday and Saturday, because that's when most of the community would come out and watch their children play; it gave them a good view of my talents when they watched our team perform. Mother told me that she grew up playing sports, and she wanted me to experience the fun as well. Sports taught me how to discipline myself and how to persevere; because even when my team was losing and things weren't going our way, we had to remain strong and finish the game. I see this form of discipline off the field as well, because when life starts to get hard, I'm reminded by my childhood emotions that I can't give up. I love everything about Phillips Park; I could smell the scent of talent coming from our opponent's dugout, and the scent of the concession stand when I was off the field. I know that place so well that I can even tell you that the swing squeaks when a kid starts to swing too high, and that there's a pathway that leads through the woods from the back of the park to a nearby neighborhood. My footprint has been on every single one of the fields at Phillips Park, for it became my stomping grounds when I showed up to show out; especially after winning the championship. We were the very first ones to win the championship for our age group on "Rainbow Day Care Center Field." After we came back from winning the championship, they put up a sign with our names on the fence at Rainbow field. Our coaches' names were Jerry, Norman, Stan, and Mike. After every game our All-Star team won, the coaches would give out stars to the key players of each game. We would take them and put them on our helmets so we could represent something even greater when we walked up to the plate. Everyone had their mom and dad cheering them on with the exception of me. You were never there to cheer me on, so I just imagined that you were in the stands beside Mother when it was my turn to step up to the plate. I played pitcher and short stop; the coaches said that I was the best fielder on the team. It was ironic, because you were never there to play catch with me, so I had to throw the ball at a brick wall and play catch with myself. I never knew what direction the ball was going to return in, so I would always be on my toes ready to catch it wherever it went. After the championship game, the coaches gave me the game ball, because I was the one who caught the last out! I was happy to have a championship trophy and the game ball, but the best trophies I have are the memories of playing baseball with a community I came to love. Regardless of what the scoreboard said, I won the experience of playing with talented players every time I stepped onto the grass diamond.

Not from Lance, but from the Heart of his Soul,

Your Child,

Lance

Chapter 6
"Family Tree Roots"

"Family Tree Roots"

I am blessed, not lucky, and I love like Casanova,

All about my green like a four leaf clover.

I thank Jehovah, and His sweet son Jesus,

For not leaving my heart shattered on the floor in pieces.

Everybody is depending on me,

Show me some R.E.S.P.E.C.T.

My responsibilities are growing bigger each day,

So I reach for a Heavenly venue and continue to pray.

I aim for perfection, but always shoot short,

I try to live like Jesus, but always fall short.

Life is too short, so stay focused to keep from losing it,

Lord be my lifeguard I'm drowning in the pulpit.

I built a life of Christ, and I tried to stop the cursing,

But I'm not perfect, I'm still under construction.

Now everybody is pointing at me; disappointed,

Sins darker than oil, I hope I'm still anointed.

I follow the Lords footsteps, so He guides my feet when I walk,

And I participate in communion so He can cleanse my tongue when I talk.

He will be my sword and my shield if I'm the last one left,

Lord be my light, as I walk through the Valley of the Shadow of Death.

Family Tree Roots

July 28, 2007

Dear Dad,

Hey Father, it's your son, Lance. It's strange that I haven't heard from you at all since my birth. I'm writing you today from a family reunion at Auntie Lene's house. I thought maybe you'd show up and I'd finally get to see you, but I'm writing this letter as a safety net just in case I thought wrong. The family reunion was dedicated to my great-grandma, Mamuka. I found out later on in life the reason why she never came by the house to see me while growing up. I came to find out that she wasn't even on earth the day I was born, well.... not physically that is. The irony ironed my soul; now it's like all of my thoughts that I pondered upon are straightforward and wrinkle free. I'm starting to see clearly through all of my blurry thoughts that lacked answers, and I'm learning more and more each day. Mother, Jada, and I now live with our grandma Mozell at our Auntie Lene's house. My Auntie Lene always makes sure that the family is molded in good shape and shampooed in good condition. Auntie Lene opens up her arms and her house to anyone in need. We've been living with them for the past three years. Grandma Mozell and Auntie Lene live out in the country, so we get to catch the bus in the mornings to go to school. Oh, and guess what dad? I'm going to finally be a teenager this year! I'm going to be turning thirteen this November. It was kind of hard playing sports and watching everyone else's dad cheer them on. I imagined you in the stands doing the same, so it didn't bother me as much when I used my creative mind to heal my hurt thoughts. By tweaking the settings of my mind, you where tattooed on my soul. Regardless of where I went, to me you were always there; and in my opinion, you were always watching my every move. I'm also going to be in high school before you know it. Time flies by faster than a flock of birds before the winter.

We were able to have custom made shirts for our Mamuka family reunion. The front of the shirts had a picture of my great-grandma Mamuka on it, and the back had a quote that read, "A family that prays together stays together." We had an amazing time with each other, but still my favorite part was stuffing my cheeks like a squirrel around a bunch of nuts! Oh my goodness.... That food was so delicious that I almost hurt myself! I guess it's just a Southern tradition to eat this good. I swear my family could own their own restaurant. I would name it "Grandma's Illicit Kitchen," because it should be illegal to cook this good. People walking by would smell the food in the air and take a detour from where they were going, like sharks when they smell blood and follow the scent. It's ironic to see how the family is connected just like a tree. Everybody is branched out in different directions, but we're still attached to the same roots which helped us grow to be on our own. We all have a different view of the world. Family reunions are beautiful, because if it wasn't for the roots of the family tree then everything else would be dead. So today's a day of dedication to our ancestors who planted the seed to our family tree. Dad I hope and pray that you decide to finally reveal your face upon me, or at least try to give a call from wherever you are. Dad, you're a branch on my family tree, but still I've never seen you. I just pray that you haven't broken off and fallen from the source.

Not from Lance, but from the Heart of his Soul,

Your Child,

Lance

Chapter 7

"High School Hormones"

"High School Hormones"

I prayed to be loved, prayed to be the one smiling and laughing,

I prayed that every girl I met wasn't a heartbreak waiting to happen.

Emotions are heavy; Hercules is too feeble to hold my feelings,

I look around, and my prayers didn't surpass the ceiling.

So I snap back to reality like I'm applauding for some poetry,

And squirt on my force field cologne so fake females can't come close to me.

These hormones are full blown, in the wind and in the soul,

I don't have to guide you through the maze, it displays a map, you know how it goes.

One week she loves you, next week she hates you,

Your career blows up, O! Now she wants to date you.

That's a coincidence, a girl like you only plays defense,

It makes no sense, how I had to reach this stage for you to engage in the offence.

Still the sex gets hot, like a jalapeño in a boiling pot, in the devils kitchen,

Don't tell me to cool down just be quiet and listen.

Every day I go to school, and I try to get an education,

Mama couldn't afford a car, so my legs were my transportation.

My girlfriends' brain is soundproof; she doesn't listen to her only parent,

Advice goes in one ear and exits out through the other,

And she looks through her mother like she's transparent.

We were young and didn't know,

That these high school hormones were out of control.

Beware when your only son's not in your sight,

You'll never know everything he participates in late at night.

We were all young and dumb, and didn't anybody know,

That these high school hormones hidden inside us were out of control.

Beware when daddy's little girl's not in his sight,

You'll never know everything your daughter does out late at night.

High School Hormones

October 23, 2010

Dear Dad,

Hey Dad, It's your son Lance. I've come to the conclusion that life isn't everything I thought it would be. It seems like people want me to live up to their expectations, and I feel like I'm limiting myself in a way. I'm in high school now, but we no longer live in the country. Auntie Lene and Mother got into an argument, so she decided to move out. We don't live in the heart of the city, but in the heart of poverty. Money is hard to come and easy to go. This place is what I think is the worst place on earth to live, but I still have a roof over my head so I guess I can't complain. We live in the projects of the inner city, and I now attend the school that holds the title for having the least amount of graduates each year. The city school system doesn't provide buses for the kids to ride, so you either drive, get a ride, or walk. With no money to purchase an extra decent vehicle, and Mother having to go to work early before the sun rises, I'm left with no choice; my legs are my only transportation. I even had to walk in the rain one time, and it so happened to be a day I forgot to put on deodorant, so yea.... I was musty to the max. I would always carry a weapon to school with me in my backpack because I trusted no one. I carried a freshly-sharpened pocket knife until I was able to upgrade to better accoutrements. I knew carrying weapons without a license was a huge risk, but from my perspective it was a defense mechanism. I saw how many people around the projects kept a gun glued to their pelvic girdle, and I refused to not be able to defend myself. Without a man in the house it made me feel like one, and from that day forward I was a completely different person. I still continue to pray every single night; although I have weapons, I pray I'll never have to use them. Dad, I hope you're happy about the person I've become, for I'm learning how to survive and become a man without an instructor. School isn't so bad once I actually make it there and get inside the building. The school only has metal detectors at the basketball games and big events, so I'm in the clear on a daily basis. Speaking of basketball.... guess what freshmen gets to play and practice with the varsity! Yes Dad, your son is a baller that girls love to lay their eyes upon. I love the respect that I get from everyone as I walk down the halls. I didn't even have to try out for the basketball team; the coach automatically put me on the team after he found out who I was related to. I have a cousin who attended the same high school, and he was a four-time All State champion! That means they won the Championship from his freshmen year to his senior year. Once the coach found out that there was another offspring from the same family tree, he didn't hesitate to ask anything.... he just put me in a jersey as fast as he could. Although I'm good at basketball, I'd rather play football because it's a way for me to take out my anger without regret. I love being on the basketball court and the football field, but still my passion is mostly put into my music and artwork. Yes Dad, your son writes lyrics on a daily basis. I would hate to call myself a rapper due to what it has become nowadays, so I'd rather call myself a soulful poet. All of the pieces I write come straight from the heart of my soul. It's like my own little world that I'm in control of. So by playing sports and writing songs, it's not a problem getting girls interested in me. They won't leave me alone, but I'm not complaining about it and I never will. I'm starting to find my taste in girls and what my taste buds prefer, and I actually have a girlfriend right now. Her name's Adrianna. She has a brown skin tone, and she's shorter than I am. I met her at the homecoming dance this year. We have so much in common that it's ridiculous. She also lives with her mother, and her father has never been in her life. She wanted to have unprotected sex with me, so I thought why not swipe my V card when I had the chance. It felt like she was the one for me, and I thought I would be with her till death do us part. I accepted it, but I know I should've used protection. Not only to prevent against pregnancy, but also due to the fact that there're many diseases in this impure world. She told me that her monthly cycle had come; I felt relieved when I heard the news that day. I made a choice that I thought you would want me to make; I thought that sex was part of becoming a man. I can only hope that I make the right choices when I see a fork in the road. If I don't try at the forks in the road, then it's going to eat me up on the inside in the future, so I'm going to try to stay off the menu. It's nerve racking undergoing these experiences without a coach who has been through it before, but I'm still learning, right? Sometimes you'll never understand things until you experience them first hand. I hope I'm making the choices you would want me to, but I can only hope, and pray.

Not from Lance, but from the Heart of his Soul,

Your Child,

Lance

Chapter 8
"Stressed Out"

"Stressed Out"

Lord pull me out this fire before it cremates me!

Tell me the reason why you devils hate me.

It's like a bottle rocket how the pistols pop off, and you can't stop it,

Everybody's killing each other like it's the new trending topic.

I'm coming up like a volcano about to erupt,

I pour my heart out so much that I might overflow your cup.

You better clean your act up, before you're officially messed up,

Ignorance is bliss, sometimes I wish I never grew up.

My roots grew deep because they threw dirt on my name,

And if I want to fly to Heaven then I must first put on these gasoline draws....

And walk through these devilish flames.

And pray to GOD I'm not cremated in the process,

When names bring fame they hunt you down like the Loch Ness.

So hunt or be hunted,

Without a doubt I'm stressed out.

Stressed Out

August 8, 2011

Dear Dad,

Oh my gosh!!! Why was I ever born? Dad, I'm weeping out to you right now! My world that I thought was going so great just turned upside down like I was on a rollercoaster without a seatbelt. I fell off from everything! I've been so frustrated and stressed lately that it doesn't even make any sense. Adrianna and I broke up over a bunch of nonsense that had nothing to do with me. I've been told that it's a slim chance I'll find the one for me at a young age; I just thought I could break the chain. Then she comes to me later saying that she's pregnant with my child! I'm still a child myself, so what am I going to do with a twin??? Mother told me not too long ago that she was pregnant again, and now it's like I'm in some kind of competition. It's going to be a hot mess if I have an offspring older than one of my siblings! It's going to be like the Rugrats in this house, or shall I say Thug rats; because we are living in the projects at the moment. Adrianna told me that her monthly cycle came so she could build up the confidence to tell me the truth. In a way, I feel it's a trick because she saw that I wasn't chasing after her from our breakup. But I'm still nervous, because I've been noticing her getting up in class to go to the restroom more and more each day. The more she rises up from her seat the further my heart sinks to my stomach. It just stresses me out and makes me sick to think that I might be a papi…. What am I to do Papi?? How would you feel if your child had a child? I knew I should've said no when she asked for unprotected sex, but I didn't and we continued to do it every time we had the chance. I don't want to say I regret it because I learned from it, but still I messed up! I just don't know how to feel about life anymore, and I'm so confused about what to do about everything. That's not even the worst part about it either! I don't know how, but my Mother found out about me being fruitful in her house! I might as well collect all my portrait photos for my obituary, because she's going to kill me! Dad, it would really make a difference if you were here right now. She had called me when school got out and told me that I was wrong for what I did.... It made me feel so awful. I started packing my bags before she got home from work, because I could see down the road where this was going to go once she got home. She knew about me being fruitful in her house, but she's clueless that there's a chance I multiplied as well. I swear, my hormones are fighting each other to the death right about now. Dad, this girl has me on a leash by putting it in my head that I put something in her. As I was packing the rest of my clothes and necessities I came across something I haven't seen in forever. I found my Boo Boo Bear that Mother gave me the day I was born. I almost started to weep as I said ignorance is bliss, for I was holding the proof. I hurried and put it back where I found it so I could continue what I was doing. A couple seconds later I heard a car pull into the driveway. Dang! She's coming whether I'm ready or not. I walked down the hallway with my heart beating fast trying to jump through my chest. As I entered the living room I heard the keys unlocking the door, and the hinges screeched as it slowly opened. Mother came into the house and stared at me as if we were having a staring contest, and she didn't utter a thought. I just walked out the house teary eyed and started to walk away from home. It was evening so the sun was starting to set; it was ironic because the daylight was running out just like my luck. It's ironic how everything we do is based upon nature. I still had money left over from school; I would design tattoos for people so I could keep a steady income of some sort. It wasn't much, but it was better than nothing. I walked to a restaurant and bought some food for the night. As I was eating, I saw a small child walk in the restaurant with only his mother, and no father. I said in my head, "Don't make the same mistakes I did kid." I'm nothing but a mistake in the making. Why am I here? I hurried and ate my food because the people in the restaurant were reminding me of my childhood. I walked out the restaurant and down the street without a destination. I thought about what Mother would have said to me and started to make my way back to the house. I guess I just needed time by myself so I would be prepared to hear her criticism on my bad decisions. I was headed home, but the rapid sound of my heartbeat made me lose track of where I was. It had got dark, and most of the streetlights around the projects were either shot off or broken. I looked behind me and noticed a silhouette of a human-like figure in the distance under one of the streetlights that still had power. I didn't know if it was a sign, someone who was after me, or just my mind playing tricks on me. So I drew my weapon ready to erase any life that came towards me, and with my eyebrows down I kept on moving. Right after I turned back around I saw a snake exit the grass and cross my path. To ensure that I would be safe, I took my weapon off safety. I looked over my shoulder and the silhouette of the human-like figure was gone, so I was a little relieved. I continued to walk looking down at the ground to see if any other creatures were near me, but when I looked up I saw the same silhouette figure in the distance straight ahead of where I was going. I knew it had to be either one of two things; my mind was playing tricks on me, or I was about to die. I took a different direction to avoid getting close to the silhouette figure, and before I knew it I saw my neighborhood in the distance. I've never been so happy to see those raggedy projects a day in my life! I put my weapon back on safety and put it back into my backpack; then I ran to Mothers' house as fast as I could. I thought about everything before I knocked on the door, and right before I was about to knock; Mother opened the door. She told me that she was waiting for me to return; she also asked, "Why did you leave?" I told her that I thought she didn't want me in her house any more. She told me that everybody makes mistakes, and I haven't done anything that hasn't been done before. I apologized and said I was sorry over and over again like a parakeet. She told me that she forgave me and to come back inside the house. I closed the door to my room and lied down on the bed. I stared at the celling watching the fan go round and round. Although Mother forgave me, I still felt bad. I started having suicidal thoughts and tried to sleep it off. I couldn't sleep so I just stared off into the darkness with my eyes bloodshot red. I said to myself, "Oh, only if I had a tour guide to walk me through the stages of life." Then I turned my speakers on and kept my eyes closed for the rest of the night. I walked on the music notes till I arrived in my own little world.

Not from Lance, but from the Heart of his Soul,

Your Child,

Lance

Chapter 9
"Mask of Makeup"

"Mask of Makeup"

Mrs. Mascara, you put on a mask because you're scared of,

If we start a relationship I might break your heart.

But I know my strength,

I know your type, and know how you think.

You can't judge a book by its cover,

So your makeup makes me wonder???

Let me read your mind,

What will I discover? What will I find?

Hiding behind trying not to be seen,

Take a sneak peek behind the scenes.

You had a bad past, and it feels like can't nobody make it up,

I feel your pain, and I can see right through your mask of makeup.

Mask of Makeup

October 27, 2012

Dear Dad,

Hey Dad, guess what I was told last year? I am not a father!!! That's all I heard replay over and over in my head. It turned out that Adrianna wasn't even pregnant. O happy day! I can't dance, but I could when I found out the news that day. Dad I was moonwalking on her front porch and everything. She waited a long time to stop lying because she knew that I didn't need her. She said she tried her best to get pregnant, because she felt like she didn't have anything of value to call her own; and a baby would've given her something to live for. It wasn't a good feeling at the time, and waiting on a pregnancy test was the longest two weeks of my life. I've learned from my bad decisions, and Adrianna is now a part of my past. I also started attending therapy to help me control my suicidal thoughts and hopefully make them stop coming all the time. My therapist is a foreign lady; so I couldn't even understand some of the questions she would ask. Not due to my lack of knowledge, but due to her speech. I really wanted my suicidal thoughts to leave my skull, so I adjusted to her accent. The first time I had a therapy session, I was provoked because somebody I've never seen before was asking me personal questions. I promise you Dad, I was almost ready to flip the table over on her head, but as time went by I got comfortable to be more open. I had to attend therapy every two weeks when I first started going, but as I got better I only had to attend once a month. Before I knew it, they told me I didn't have to come anymore. My confidence was back and I started forgetting about my sessions. It's a good feeling to know that you have your head on straight again. I now have a different view on the world, but still I don't know everything. My situation with Adrianna was my biggest mistake so far, and believe it or not, she still tries to come back into my life. She even tried asking my mother if she could baby sit my newborn siblings. Yea I said newborn; I have two new siblings now. I have another little sister name Destiny and a baby brother name Makhi. They both have the same dad, but still I'm the older brother that all my siblings are going to look up to. Adrianna has gone too far just to try and come back into my life! Still to this day Mother doesn't know about the pregnancy scare I experienced with her, but as long as it wasn't true that's all that matters....right? I've moved on to better things, for I now know the do's and don'ts of being in relationships. Speaking of relationships, I've found somebody else who could provide shelter for my heart; her name is Valerie. I met her at this year's homecoming dance. It's ironic how I meet all my partners in crime around the same time each year, and at the same place! A new song had just started playing, and I saw a girl with long black hair standing beside the crowd. The lights were off, so I couldn't see her face beyond her beautiful black hair. The first words I said to her were, "Excuse me miss, may I have this dance?" After dancing for a few minutes we tried to talk, but we couldn't hear each other over the loud music. I knew Valerie was different from all the other girls I met at the dance, because she was the only girl I danced with who didn't dance like a stripper. Valerie gave me her number, but after that I lost her in the crowd. I ignored all the girls who tried to throw themselves at me, because I was thinking of Valerie for the rest of the night. I called her the next morning and we talked for hours, it was almost like we connected as soon as we heard each other's voices. She was telling me how her mother never allowed her to wear makeup, but last night was the first time she tried on a mask of powder. It was kind of weird because I was a little tipsy the night before, plus the lights were off at the dance, so I don't know what she actually looks like. My birthday is coming up soon next month, so maybe then I'll get to see what she actually looks like and learn more about her. We're not actually in a relationship yet, but I can feel the anchor of her soul slowly letting down her emotions onto me.

Not from Lance, but from the Heart of his Soul,

Your Child,

Lance

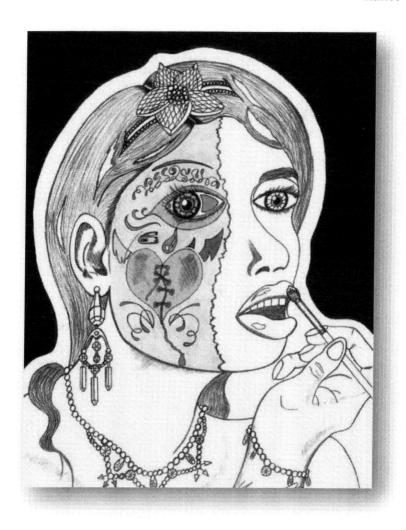

Chapter 10
"Faithful to Your Female"

"Faithful to Your Female"

There are stitches on my heart; the reason being, I'll never fear it,

I needed a woman of knowledge to feed me the fruits of the spirit.

My heart's a Cherokee water drum when ignorance is bliss,

We kiss; until the sun sets and our lips go numb.

When one thing goes numb you have to replace it,

Place it in a place where you're sure it can fit; and feel,

I need a strait jacket because I can't sit still;

It's like the Fourth of July how fireworks pop off between you and I.

She's faithful to me; vice versa; I'm faithful to her,

The only place we talk about something is where it occurs.

I'm her life size teddy bear; my cutie can't bear to snuggle and cuddle,

I'll wet up my leather jacket just so she won't step in a puddle.

My heart is her heart; her heart is my heart;

And when we make love we craft a unique art.

My favorite part will be when I add a wedding ring to my shopping cart.

When I come around; her biggest challenge is to not make a sound,

When your child gets older the bedroom becomes their playground.

When I'm antisocial, I'll talk to your soul and your soul only,

That's when she called my phone and said you don't have to be lonely.

I'm right here with you, and I'll never forget you,

And I'll never regret the moment we met; plus the times we've had,

I chose to be shot by Cupid because your love is all I have.

I'll be faithful to you if you be faithful to me.

Faithful to Your Female

November 10, 2012

Dear Dad,

Hey Dad, guess what day it is today? It's my birthday again; nowadays I'm thankful just to see the next day. If I wake up in the morning, there's no reason why I should complain about anything, because there's someone who doesn't wake up to see the light of life. So Dad, regardless of where you are and regardless of what's going on, if you at least wake up then try to make a difference in the world. I try to see the bright side of every situation, and I've learned that a positive mind can take me far. We no longer live in the projects anymore! In the name of Jesus I proudly say Thank You! Mother decided to move back in with Grandma Mozell and Auntie Lene, so I no longer attend that devil's playground of a high school. I turned 18 years old today; you know what that means, I'm a legal adult now. I can't get into any fights or anything now, because if they put me in handcuffs, I don't think the Juvie is going to be my destination. It's time to get smarter and adjust my adolescent mind for adulthood. Today was an awesome day, and I had a great time at my party I didn't know I was going to have.

Mother threw a surprise party for me today, and it really caught me off guard! I woke up thinking that we weren't going to do anything for my birthday, it felt like another regular day to me. At first, Mother was telling me that I needed to go to the barbershop because I looked like a wooly mammoth; she kept saying that it might be a good idea to hurry up and go. I didn't catch on to anything yet, but I still went to get a haircut. When I returned to home, I sat down on the couch to rest a little. Then Mother came into the room and kept telling me that it would be a good idea to take a shower as well. I said alright, but I didn't go

ASAP. After a while I heard someone knocking on the door. It was some of my family members with birthday bags asking me why I didn't have on any decent clothes for my party. I told them I didn't know I was having a party, and behind them I saw a black truck pull up that has never visited my house before. Out hops the most beautiful piece of Heaven I've ever laid eyes upon. It was Valerie in the daytime! She's light skinned with long black hair, and none of its weave! She appears to be shorter than me as well. I actually saw her for the first time and she's drop dead gorgeous! Then my senses told me that I still needed a shower because I had hair all over me from my haircut, so I hurried and ran inside before she could see me. Dad I promise that was the fastest shower I've ever taken, and I've never scrubbed myself that hard before. After I got dressed to impress I noticed many more people in my house ready to eat and have a great time. I saw Valerie sitting on the couch not talking to anyone; it was ironic because we would talk forever over the phone. I walked over and asked if the seat beside her was taken, she said it was up to me. I told her it's my house anyway so I sit where I please. We hugged each other and started talking for a little while. Valerie started to get quiet and I asked her what was wrong; she told me that she was shy! I told her to make herself at home because whatever is mine can be hers if she wants it to be. I brought her some food from the kitchen, and she said I read her mind. As we kept talking, she told me that her mom had passed away a few years back due to breast cancer; and she was still having trouble dealing with the transition. That explained why she never wore a mask of makeup before, because her mom didn't want her to hide her true beauty. She told me that it all happened on the fourth of December, and she was still petrified of that specific date. I told her that she could call me at any time of the day and anytime of the night. I wanted her to know that she can be comfortable around me, for I've always been faithful to my females regardless of what they may have done. That's when she leaned over to me and gave me our very first kiss.

Not from Lance, but from the Heart of his Soul,

Your Child,

Lance

Chapter 11
"Sweet Tooth"

"Sweet Tooth"

Her lips are sweet like cotton candy, and softer than cotton,

She spoils me till I'm rotten.

She says I've been stressing; lays me on my back and tells me to relax,

She has my heartbeat doing jumping jacks.

I think I'm addicted; if I were to be convicted,

I would go loco craving for your body you know.

Craving like a fiend; I'm going to fulfill all your fantasy dreams.

It begun when your sweetness rolled off the tip of my tongue,

I need a brown paper bag for my hyperventilating lungs.

From the top of cloud nine I fell from above,

Then your love caught me like a baseball glove.

They say pleasure turns to pain; and that's how it is,

A lot of pain from all of the pleasure that is.

Her lips are sweeter than candy; so good you won't find it in a store,

She leaves me relaxed to the max and begging for more.

Sweet Tooth

November 17, 2012

Dear Dad,

Hey Dad, it's a week after my birthday and Valerie already wants to spend more time with me. It's like we got a taste of what it's like to be around each other, and now we have a sweet tooth for each other. I call her every morning before she goes to school to let her know I'm always there for her. She invited me over to go meet her family today, and she said that they loved my visit. Before I arrived, she told me that her dad had a shotgun ready for me when I got there, me being myself, I told her to tell him to make sure that it was loaded. I automatically showed her father what type of person I was before I even got there. My eyes were wide open when I arrived at her home, you couldn't miss it because it was the biggest house in the neighborhood. When I rang the doorbell, I met her father for the very first time. He retired from the military and now works for the government. He is his own boss, and he inspired me when he didn't even know it. I always wanted to grow up to be a successful man, and Valerie's dad showed me that it was possible if I remained consistent. We had dinner and Valerie treated me to a great visit. Before I left we talked some more about how we felt about each other. She had become my inspiration for doing everything to the best of my ability. I wanted to provide everything for her and give her the life of a queen. I knew in my heart that there was a high possibility that she was the one for me, but only time could tell. She wasn't as mature as I was so she didn't understand my train of thought so well. I still continued to love her with all my heart and all my soul, just how a real man is supposed to. After I left her house, I noticed that she watched me from the door until she could no longer see me down the road. I called her when I got home so she would know that I made it home safely. I know how it is when you have feelings for someone and they don't communicate with you; it turns into corruption because communication is everything in a relationship. I had to learn that the hard way because people often start to change when you think you're both on the same page. Mother tells me that I fall in love too easily, but what would you expect if there was no one to teach me how to level out the different stages of love? I was given a heart and a soul, so I'm going to use them both to comfort the girl I have feelings for. I don't know if I'm making the right decision, but I'm going to show her that I have love for her through my actions. Although I'm writing this letter, my actions will always speak louder than the ink on the paper. Dad, did you treat your females like queens when they couldn't see their crowns?

Not from Lance, but from the Heart of his Soul,

Your Child,

Lance

Chapter 12

"Broken Hearts and Shattered Dreams"

"Broken Hearts and Shattered Dreams"

Broken hearts, shattered dreams,

One of the sharp pieces made you fall from the balance beam.

So I gave you my heart, but you misused it,

Now I keep it all on display in the museum of my music.

Far away from the world,

I untied that noose from around your neck and gave you
diamonds and pearls.

I couldn't sleep and count sheep as a kid, but when I did,

I think the Sandman built a sand castle on my eyelids.

Because I could picture Heaven, and I could see my future,

And I could picture paparazzi taking pictures of me.

Women stop and stare up at me like UFO's in the night,

Blinded by my future like a deer caught in some headlights.

Don't swerve into the ditches,

The GPS system could never pick up on this road to riches.

Even a cat with nine lives is clueless of its fate,

So if I don't make it into Heaven then just let me be a hobo by
the gates.

So I can thank my ancestors for planting the seed to my family
tree,

Because it sprouted and provided shade for me.

Broken Hearts and Shattered Dreams

November 19, 2012

Dear Dad,

Dad I can't seem to understand why everyone wants me to live up to their expectations; it makes me feel like I'm limiting myself from what I'm capable of doing. How am I going to be where I want in life if everyone around me wants me to do what they think is best for me? I feel like I'm taking a detour from the path of my dreams, a detour from what I was sent here to do. People think that I'm not progressing in anything just because I isolate myself from everybody else. When the reason I isolated myself is so that I can continue to water my talents and watch them grow. I feel like my family is starting to look at me different, and it's all because they don't understand my train of thought. My English teacher once told me, "To be misunderstood is to be great." You're misunderstood because your perspective is a vision that the world has yet to see. It's like judging a movie by the actors, or a book by its cover. I just want them to leave me alone and let me be myself, so then I can be able to move out of the house faster than your ordinary young adult. I feel like they don't believe in my dreams anymore, if they ever did. People are always telling me that the field of entertainment I want to go in is a one in a million chance. Provoked inside; I say to myself.... Have they ever thought I was that one in a million? I don't care about whom else in the world does what I want to do, I'm worried about myself, and myself only! I refuse to sit around and waste time pondering my precious thoughts on what other people do, or what other people have to say about me. People can talk about me all they want, for they talked about Jesus when He was living, and not in a good way. We're supposed to follow in His footsteps. So if people have so much to say about me, then that lets me know that I'm on the right track. People are going to talk about you till the day you die, and if you ignore them then your name will still be the topic of discussion afterwards. It used to tilt my self-esteem off balance when I was younger, but now it motivates me when people tell me it's a slim chance and I'm not going to make it. There will be power in my hands the day I prove them wrong. To see that day sooner, I focus on what I need to accomplish and not on revenge, for it will come in the package of success. I try to teach Valerie a better way of viewing the world, but she always lets her self-esteem get the best of her. She is the complete opposite from me when it comes to self-esteem. I never understand why she cares about what people think of her, if she would just listen to me then she wouldn't have those problems. You can walk a thirsty horse to the river, but you can't make it drink from the water. Mainly what I'm saying is that you can't help anybody who doesn't want any help. If people ignore your advice, then just forget about it and continue to focus on yourself, for if you don't, then it'll just be a mound of sand on the floor; a lot of time wasted. I'm done living up to everyone's expectations; I'm going to follow my dreams, and if it turns out that my life is a suicide mission, I'll know that I at least helped and blessed someone before I took the fall for a better chance. I've never been a selfish soul. Dad, am I living up to your expectations of a man?

Not from Lance, but from the Heart of his Soul,

Your Child,

Lance

Chapter 13
"Previews of the Pain"

"Previews of the Pain"

You tried to slowly push me away, and depart us like continental drift,

But I'm still holding on to you like you're hanging from a cliff.

I'm holding on to my love,

Because I refuse to give up on an angel that the Lord sent from above.

Actions speak louder than words,

And you're not answering the phone or even texting me one word.

You feel as if you're incarcerated in the darkness I know,

And when you don't have a flashlight just remember that every angel has their halo.

It glows, and I can see it from a million miles away,

I'll probably mistake it for the lucent moon one day.

Just remember to pray,

And know that there's a reason why you are still breathing today.

All throughout the day, I cry out that I need you,

I said I'd provide for you, so don't bite the hand that feeds you.

I feel nauseous because I'm on this rollercoaster called life,

Regardless of our ups and downs, everything is going to be alright.

I know it may seem all wrong, but we've been holding on for so long,

Lance Brazelton

I feel passion in your presence, and we're not singing the same song.

I know you wept a river for your mom; I swam through it to make it to you today,

So wrap your beauty in my arms, and strive off of the strong things she would say.

Previews of the Pain

December 1, 2012

Dear Dad,

Hey Dad, It's your son Lance. It's getting close to the time of year that Valerie's mother passed away. Valerie told me that she had passed on the fourth of December a couple of years ago. I noticed that it's the core of her pain that her self-esteem issues orbit around. I try to encourage her to focus on making her mother happy, but whatever I say just goes in one ear and out the other. I guess it's just expected, because we're still not officially in a relationship yet. It's like she only hears what she wants to hear; that doesn't mean I should stop trying, right? She told me that she had a dream last night about her mother. She was telling me how she would wake them up and get them ready for school every single morning. She would make them all pray before they left the house, showing them the strength of a strong Christian woman. Valerie said that even after she found out that she had breast cancer, she would still get up and work as though nothing was wrong. She always would make sure that she was flawless from head to toe before she left the house. People didn't even know she had breast cancer because she would always be the most beautiful woman in every room she entered. Valerie called me in the middle of the night because she couldn't stop thinking about the dream. I tried to comfort her, but it's hard when she never listens or allows my advice to walk into her brain. It's like what I'm saying is knocking on her skull waiting to be greeted by her melancholy thoughts. I think it's because those melancholy thoughts know that they wouldn't survive against my advice from the soul; I guess that's an explanation for why she doesn't listen. Her dream was like a preview for how she's going to feel in three days. I prayed with her and told her that I would stay on the phone while she went back to sleep. I hope that she finally starts listening to my advice so she can see a brighter day. She has cried too many times at night to not be smiling during the day. I pray that it doesn't hit her as bad in the coming three days. Dad, how am I supposed to be there for the girl I love when you never taught me how to balance out a woman's emotions?

Not from Lance, but from the Heart of his Soul,

Your Child,

Lance

Chapter 14
"The 4th of December"

"The 4th of December"

Your heart has a cast and a crutch; I cannot say much about how
you feel,

The battle wound is too deep; it's a cut that only GOD's touch
can heal.

It's so much stress on my chest, and it hurts when I cough,

This world spins like a carnival ride; stop it, I want to get off.

A mine is planted on my mind, now it's so hard to think,

I used to be asking for miracles, but now I'm asking for strength.

Life is not a movie, but after death is the sequel;

Heaven is a prepared place, for prepared people.

Tell your dad I respect him, and I would never disrespect you,

I know he doesn't trust me, he just met me, I don't expect him
to.

I'm not the villain, for I am a man of Amen,

His wife taught me that the world's filled with phenomenal
women.

I have amour for you and all of your siblings,

Every day's Thanksgiving for me because I'm thankful for you.

You've been weeping for years, but in Heaven they're rejoicing
in cheers,

You're stronger and no longer have to play tug of war with your
tears.

Because it's okay! And do not worry,

Just keep ya head up and keep praying for me.

And when you see my face; remember that I'm in a perfect place,

Where the happiness I draw cannot be erased.

I don't have to stress no more, don't have to hurt no more,

The road is not rougher because I don't suffer anymore.

I don't have to cry no more; don't have to die no more,

And I don't walk through any rain because my pain is
nevermore....

The 4th of December

December 4, 2012

Dear Dad,

Hey Dad, today's the day that Valerie prepares herself for every year. I called her early this morning and she was talking in a low tone for the very first time. I was telling her that her mother wouldn't want her to cry and be upset because she's in a better place now. Valerie told me that her mom wore a bracelet that prevented people from helping her. I told her that maybe she felt that if it was her time then it was just her time. But to her, everything I said was a bunch of nothing; words without sound. I knew that she wouldn't listen to anything I tried to tell her, so I took a different approach. I decided to write her a heartfelt song about her mother. I wrote it as quick as I could so I could touch her heart as soon as possible; I knew that she would feel better the second I put it in her hand. I drew an illustration to go along with the message that I was trying to tell her. I put it in a nice hard folder so it wouldn't get wet; it just so happened to be raining that day, Ironic? When I arrived at her home, I prepared myself to give her my heart in the palm of my hands, because I put all my heart into everything I write. When I gave it to her, she started crying before she even opened it. She wouldn't stop crying so I held her in my arms as I read it to her. For the first time she listened to everything I said and didn't interrupt me not one time. I wiped her tears from her twinkling eyes and told her that she didn't have to cry anymore because everything was okay. She gave me the most soulful look and told me that she loved me. I gave her a kiss on her cute little cheek and told her that she could always come to me for anything. When I arrived back at home, guess who was there out of all people.... Adrianna! I didn't say anything about Valerie because I wasn't in the mood for any nonsense. She told me that she wanted to come visit my grandma and see how my family was doing. I didn't say anything other than, "That's fine." I don't wish anything but the best for Adrianna, and all I can do is pray for her at this point; because I have to do what's best for myself. I walked out the room while she was talking to my grandma. I sat in the living room and continued to work on some songs that I almost had finished. When she was about to leave I noticed that she went towards my room assuming I was in there, I didn't say a word. When she saw I wasn't in there, she came through the living room and gave me a hug while I was sitting on the couch; I told her to be safe on the way home. I was a little confused of why she would show up out of nowhere, and today of all days. I guess people can just sense your soul when you're being yourself. You'll see more and more people on your front porch when you're not thinking about them. At the end of the day I called my beautiful Valerie to see how she was doing before she fell asleep. I didn't say anything about Adrianna coming over out of nowhere because it wasn't important. If I can prevent Valerie from thinking about stuff she doesn't have to, then I will, because we only need to focus on the things that will help us grow in the world. She told me that the song I wrote made her feel better about herself, and she looked at things from a different perspective. I prayed with her and stayed on the phone until she went to sleep. After she fell asleep, I prayed that I continued to use my talents to help the wounded. I love my life, and I just hope that the thoughts I put in Valerie's head never fade like an old picture, for I never know how long these happy feelings will make her smile. Dad, does it make you smile knowing that I made a positive change in a girls' life?

Not from Lance, but from the Heart of his Soul,

Your Child,

Lance

Chapter 15
"I Amor You"

"I Amor You"

Excuse me Miss, may I have this dance?

My name is Lance, and I'm not trying to get in your pants.

I'm trying to get to know you, study you, and learn to love you,

So you can learn to love me for the soul within me.

We're not in Paris, but we're French kissing,

I can make you think love is my invention,

And did I mention her favorite position,

Will be the one when I get down on one knee,

And ask her to marry me!

Last December our ship had set sail,

So we walked the plank to drown in the pool of love we poured
for each other.

My eyes are like dark clouds, and when it rains it pours,

My tears splash against the ground while I hold your hands and
wipe yours.

Your face is an amazing grace, and I cannot believe,

You caught me by the eye, no apple, Adam or Eve.

Every day I hope and pray I'm getting closer to your heart,

I kiss you through the phone like a kid; I guess I needed
somewhere to start.

Today is a gift; is that why we call it the present?

My soul is happy in his heart if I shed a tear in your presence.

You don't need a mask of makeup to remain top notch,

You make my heart skip a beat like he's playing hop scotch.

You can take away my home; incarcerate me all alone,

Long as I see you in my mind I'm the happiest man of all time.

In a dark world of downfall you'll be my lucent rising star,

I wish to Amor you more,

Like the pretty princess that you are.

I Amor You

December 14, 2012

Dear Dad,

Hey Dad, guess who officially has a new girlfriend again....
Valerie and I made our relationship official. I asked her out after
the schools' basketball game. Before we got in the car, I told her
that I needed to ask her something. I got down on one knee like
I was about to ask her to marry me, just acting silly and being
myself. After I stood back up I hugged her and asked her if I could
make her mine. She started crying as she was saying yes to my
question. She looked at me after she answered the question, and
I've never seen a more passionate look on Valerie's face before.
We passionately kissed each other from the depths of our hearts
before we entered the car. Valerie called me later on that night
before she went to sleep, and we talked until she fell asleep on the
phone. I guess my voice is soothing and relaxing to her, or I might
just be flat out boring.... We started to spend more time with each
other as we learned more about one another. She says that she has
told me everything about her, but I can only know what she tells
me. Some people just tell you what they want you to know so you
don't have second thoughts about them. I just hope that I'm able
to trust Valerie when my back's against the wall and she's the only
one who can hear my cry for help. When you first start a brand
new relationship, you don't really know everything about that
person, for only time can reveal who they truly are. I don't want
another repeat of what happened with my first love, so I'm going
to take it as slow as the drift of the ocean. Maybe we'll grow old
together like the Veterans of Love.

Oh yeah Dad, speaking of the Veterans of Love. One of
my cousins on Mother's side of the family got married not too
long ago. Her wedding was held in Birmingham, so we took a trip

out of town to help her celebrate. Everyone at the wedding knew about my poetry and music, so they requested a spoken word from me. I recited a poem that I wrote in the inspiration of Valerie and me becoming one. My newly wedded cousin loved the poem so much that she started to cry towards the end. One plus one equals one, but that's only if you're honest to your true love. If one person is not whole and does not have themselves together, then they'll never match up to their partner who's ready to take the next step. You must be adjacent with each other mentally, and most importantly spiritually. Only time can tell you if you made the right decisions. When everything is sweet you must remember that life is a pattern of problems, and your heart's the golden calculator that can solve them. I don't know if I'm on the right track, but I do know that I'm going to love hard. Whether its success or failure, I know I'm preparing myself for something. Dad, how can I know if I'm making the right decisions?

Not from Lance, but from the Heart of his Soul,

Your Child,

Lance

Chapter 16
"My Fate"

"My Fate"

What is my fate?

Is it a force that guides me through?

Or is it just a sign that will leave me down and blue?

Does it decide exactly what happens to me?

Or does it pick out exactly what I'm destined to be?

These are all good questions, but will they ever be answered?

That's the number one question at the top of the list.

Will I continue to exist when my life comes to a dead end?

I pray to live a life in Heaven so the peace can begin?

I try to live like Jesus; is that why it feels like I'm living just to die?

My tears fall like water from a faucet; can anybody tell me why?

Majority of the world hates me; I wonder if a small portion loves me to death,

I wanted to tell ya'll I amor you before I exhale my last breath.

I'm buried deep under depression, and I'm strangled by stress,

I throw a smoke bomb in my lungs to get it off of my chest.

Depression hits you so deep, you hear the demons tip toe when they creep,

And you toss and turn your emotions while trying to go to sleep.

I pray to the Lord my soul to take,

Because it's not guaranteed that I will awake.

My Fate

January 1, 2013

Dear Dad,

Hey Dad, once again another Christmas has gone by, but still no sign of where you could be or what you may be thinking. I wonder if you think about me at all, or do you already know about everything somehow? Today was the start of a brand new year, and my New Year's resolution was to fulfill my purpose in life.... Whatever that job may be. Grandma Mozell and Auntie Lene cooked some black eyed peas and hog jowls; they say you have to eat it on the first day of a new year for good luck. Auntie Lene's husband, my Uncle Hayward, wasn't feeling so well while we were celebrating New Year's, so he stayed in their room while we were giving each other a toast. Later that night Uncle Hayward had a stroke and Auntie Lene had to rush him to the hospital. Auntie Lene would call us from time to time to keep us informed about what was going on. Black eyed peas and hog jowls were supposed to mean good luck for the year, and I'm not seeing that at all because it's still the first day of the year. I feel like I'm in the irony of the world. Every time I think something's going good, there's always a twist that pulls me in the opposite direction. If I was never born then I wouldn't have to deal with anything. In a sense, it feels like my family isn't who I really thought they were. As a child, I always looked up to them thinking that there wasn't anyone else in the world who I could learn from. Now I realize that everything I've learned has come from mistakes and experiences, now my family is starting to fall apart. Everyone in the house stays to themselves and rarely shares conversations like they used to. I don't know if this is a sign of something about to happen, or just my family becoming antisocial. No one sees my point of view on anything. They assume that I'm not focused on anything because they never see me while I'm working. I don't want to say that I hate my life, but at this point I don't think there's any other order I can arrange these words. The older I get, the more I realize how selfish this cruel world really is. Dad, I could go on forever telling you how much evil there is walking on the face of this earth. With Uncle Hayward getting sick, I think there's something trying to make its way inside our home. I've been having this strange feeling lately, and the sun rarely shines now. I'll never know the future, so I can only ponder my lonely questions with what I think will happen. I pray that the reason will always be for the best, but I can only pray because my fate is still a mystery.

Not from Lance, but from the Heart of his Soul,

Your Child,

Lance

Chapter 17
"A Missing Puzzle Piece"

"A Missing Puzzle Piece"

I once heard my Auntie Say, "I might not be here tomorrow, so I'm going to have fun today."

We sometimes laugh to replace the times that we weep,

I no longer have to drop teardrop bombs, for you are resting peacefully in eternal sleep.

Look out below! Because my tears still fall,

Like the golden brown leaves in the middle of Fall.

As I grow older, growing pains grow through my veins like a virus,

My eyes are bloodshot red, and I don't have conjunctivitis.

Never again will you have to breathe this air of sin,

Sit back and relax while we take care of the children.

I amour you Auntie, and vice-versa, you amour me,

When you're made in GOD's image it's impossible to be ugly.

I know we're going to make it regardless of what we have to go through,

I remember you telling me if I stay focused then my dreams will come true....

My ladybug puzzle is missing a piece, even though it's not complete,

The struggle still made me unique and antique.

All I see are question marks, because all I do is ask "Why?"

The bright side of your death is more like a star in the sky;

I pray that it twinkles like the faith in my grandmas eyes.

When the clouds hung low, GOD moved them out the way,

Changed the weeping into laughter, and the darkness into day.

Johanna is beautiful, well, she's Auntie Lene to me,

She will never be nevermore, like the waves in the sea.

So when this life comes to an end I'll know exactly where to start,

I found the missing puzzle piece deep in the depths of my heart.

It was never lost.

A Missing Puzzle Piece

January 12, 2013

Dear Dad,

I pray that you please order her steps and spread her beautiful wings. Dad, my Auntie Lene has flown away to a better place. I know that she's going to be safe, but it still hurts when you're trying to adjust to something new, and you've been adapted to what you knew as a child for so long. It all started when I was about to go to sleep late after a long night of writing. I was lying in bed when I thought I heard someone yelling for help; I thought I was dreaming so I continued to sleep. I had noticed that the cries for help continued to go beyond the walls of our home. I quickly got out of bed and followed the cries that were desperately asking for help, and it led to my Auntie Lene's room. When I entered I saw Uncle Hayward on the floor holding my Auntie Lene in his arms. He was still sick from his stroke, and he hasn't been able to walk. He said that she had passed out and hit her head on the corner of her antique table. He wasn't able to walk at all, and just the fact that he found the strength to crawl over to her and hold her head in his arms.... it made me cry. It was the most beautiful expression of love I've ever seen in my life! After I woke everyone else up and told them what had happened, the only thing we could do was call 911. When paramedics arrived, they tried to perform CPR on my Auntie Lene, but there was no sign of a pulse. The paramedics had to resort to the defibrillator and hope for a pulse while I prayed for one. As they shocked my Auntie Lene, I couldn't do anything but watch as the police lights flashed upon the tears sprinting down my face. They still couldn't get a pulse started in my Auntie, so I walked away from the scene that I could no longer bear to watch. I called my Mom and told her what was going on. She couldn't clearly hear what I was saying; it sounded like I was under water because I was about to drown in my own tears. The paramedics quickly put my Auntie Lene on a stretcher and took her out through her room's porch that Hayward built for her. The porch by their room was filled with tons of puzzles that Auntie Lene completed throughout her life. Auntie Lene loved to complete puzzles with over a thousand pieces to them. After we got her in the ambulance, I just stared at all of the puzzles on her porch, and it felt as though I could feel everything she was thinking while putting them together. Uncle Hayward cried his eyes out as he sat in the room that he built for her with his own two hands. I couldn't do anything but pray that she would be alright. Our whole family decided to meet at the hospital a few days after the incident. As I was sitting in the back seat, I heard Grandma Mozell tell Mother that they were going to pull the plug on Auntie Lene if she continued to descend away from progress, because they knew she would want them to do it. I asked Mother if Auntie Lene was going to be okay, and she said that there were multiple things wrong with her. She told me that she had a heart attack and there were multiple seizures taking place in her brain, and all at one time. The doctor said that even if she did live through it, then she would have to be taken care of for the rest of her life because her brain was so critically damaged. Auntie Lene's daughter, my cousin Natalie, said that she didn't want her mother to suffer with all of the pain anymore. My family decided to pull the plug.... I was one of the people who was able to be in the room while everything was going on. After the doctor pulled the plug, my Auntie Lene continued to breathe on her own, but I didn't know if she was doing it herself. I stood up and prayed the whole time while the hours went by like minutes. I think Auntie Lene continued to breathe because she didn't want me to watch her exhale her last breath. I thought to myself that if I woke up earlier the morning of the incident, then maybe she would still be here with us. I cried my eyes out like I was a newborn again. When I hugged Auntie Lene for the last time with air in her lungs, I felt her angel wings wrapping around me, and I felt her soul hug mine.

At that very moment, I promised her that I was going to take care of our family, regardless of the cost. When I walked away from her hospital room, I asked myself the same question over and over again, "Was she proud of me? Was she proud of me? Was she proud of me?" Mother looked me in my eyes and said, "Why would she not be proud of her talented nephew?" Auntie Lene helped raise me from an infant, and she was there when there was no father figure to tuck me in at night. I thought to myself that losing her would be like losing a portion of my heart, because she was that one puzzle piece that held us all together. I went home later that night to help with my little siblings, so Mother could go back up to the hospital with the rest of the family. All throughout that night I prayed in a puddle of tears. The next morning I woke up to the sound of the house phone ringing. When I answered I heard them say, "This is Royal Funeral Home, and we wanted to let you know that Mrs. Johanna Brazelton (Auntie Lene) arrived this morning." I hung up without saying a word.... I looked at my little sister and burst into tears as I uttered the words, "The funeral home has Auntie Lene now." When I received that phone call it came to my senses that she was really gone. Right after I hung up the phone, Grandma Mozell and Mother had just arrived back home. Soon as they walked in the door they said that she didn't make it. I couldn't do anything but stare at the twinkle of strength that they held in their eyes. I could tell that they really wanted to break down, but they didn't so we wouldn't be upset. I knew there was a dark rain cloud in the house when we were not at home. Valerie and her dad came by to bring us food and they checked on us. I've never seen so much chicken in my life! When people came over to visit, I could tell they were trying to laugh to keep from crying. Everyone had wanted me to write a poem for Auntie Lene, and I put it in her obituary because I knew I wouldn't be able to recite it at her funeral. I named it "A Missing Puzzle Piece." I knew how much she loved puzzles, and it felt like a piece was actually missing from my heart. I knew that everything would never be the same again. Auntie Lene not only paid for everything, but she also made sure that everyone in the house was alright. Since then I've kept my emotions to myself because no one else would understand my point of view on anything. Now I search inside my soul when I'm working on my writing. Maybe one day I'll find that missing puzzle piece to patch up the empty space where my love once lived. I continue to search for that one missing puzzle piece. Dad, am I the one missing puzzle piece that's keeping your life from becoming complete?

Not from Lance, but from the Heart of his Soul,

Your Child,

Lance

Chapter 18
"The Color of My Skin"

"The Color of My Skin"

If Martin Luther King didn't chase his dream,

We would still be segregated, and separated into teams.

Everything in black & white like TV in the fifties,

This whole world is color blind, by the color of our skin.

You're supposed to be my brother,

We both bleed blood, so why do you judge us by our color?

Slavery is over but we're still hung by the rope,

At the end dangling before I pass away I hope,

GOD forgives me, for leaving the clip empty,

When it's kill or be killed you tell me what would you do?

And what would Jesus do? W.W.J.D.

I'm only human so it doesn't work that easy for me.

We shed tears for many years, and we're still not extinct,

Because you can't wipe away the tears tatted in black ink.

The color of my skin had to fight for our rights,

And still to this day I'm trying to fight for what's right.

I'm a freedom fighter, so all my soldiers raise your fist higher,

Don't cry, testify! And tell the world how you feel.

You don't have to like me, and you don't have to love me,

You're not my GOD with the gavel so you cannot judge me.

So don't judge me again, by the color of my skin.

Lance Brazelton

The Color of My Skin

February 7, 2013

Dear Dad,

Hey Dad, it's Black History month; the shortest month of the year, ironic isn't it? I see a lot of old-time films come on around this time. I remember last year during Black History month a seventeen year old kid was shot in Florida because of the color of his skin. He was wearing a black hoodie when he was shot. After his death, a lot of people started wearing black hoodies to school, and I was one of them. The kid was shot wearing a black hoodie, and I envisioned the shooter wearing a white hoodie, just like the KKK. It's ironic how the KKK came to mind, because they would kill black people because of the color of their skin; and the shooter participated in the same exact act.... over half a century later. I pray that another situation like that will never happen again. Every single year we have a Black History month program at our school to celebrate what Black History means to us. I never actually participated in the Black History month program until this year. My life connections teacher was going to be hosting the show. One day after class she had asked to speak with me, and she asked me if I wanted to be in the Black History month program; because she knew how passionate I was about writing. She asked if I could write a poem to recite; I told her if I'm going to be on stage then I might as well perform a song. When I went home that night, I got started on it as soon as I could, because there was only one week before the show. I put myself in the state of mind that I was actually living during slavery, and then told it from a present point of view. After I mixed the music to the piece, I gave it a powerful title, "The Color of My Skin." I had the song produced, wrote, and memorized in less than one week. We went through the Black History month program a day before the show. My teacher heard what I created for the first time, and she loved it! She told me that there was something inside me that needs to be shown to the world, and it made me feel like I was actually worth something. When the day of the show came, I dressed up for school like I was about to perform at the BET Awards. I didn't talk to anyone that morning at school, because I was only focused on the message that I had to recite from my soul. I didn't care if I only touched one person, as long as I can save one person with my words then it was all worth it. The end of the school day was about to come, and the performers were released from class to get ready for the Black History month program. As I entered the auditorium, I felt like I was about to fly into the bright lights in the upper deck. I could hear the auditorium filling up as I waited back stage. As the roaring crowd grew louder in numbers, I got more confident about the message I was about to recite. When the performers before me did their acts, I didn't talk to anyone. I was there for only one reason; to be myself, and touch every soul I could while on stage. I heard them announce my name, and then they started the intro to my piece…. This is why I'm here at this very moment with a microphone in my hand. I started thinking about my Auntie Lene while my intro was still playing, because I knew that she was watching me. "Auntie, I pray that I make you proud." The spotlight enhanced the twinkle in my eyes as I stepped onto the stage. During the first verse I could hear people clapping along to the rhythm of my music as they listened to what I had to say. After the chorus of the song, I could hear people screaming my name and cheering me on. Performing is one of the best feelings I've ever had, because it felt like people were finally listening to what I had to say. After the third verse, I went out into the crowd while the music was still playing. The crowd was screaming their lungs out so loud that I couldn't even hear my music anymore, but oh well; I just continued to talk with the rhythm I heard in my head. Before the song was over, I started to cry for some reason. I think it was because I felt my Auntie Lene cheering me on from Heaven. When my performance was finished, I could still hear the crowd saying my name while I was back stage. The school principals said that it was because of students like me that made Lee High School the best school in the region. I love the feeling of knowing that I touched many people with the words from my heart. They loved it so much that another school principal asked us to do the program for his school. And after that I was requested to perform at colleges and churches, it felt like I was on tour for this one song, a song that I did in less than one week! I was even requested to perform my song after Black History month was over! The impact of my words made everyone want to hear what I had to speak about next, but that's a question that I ask myself every day.... What's next??? Dad, how can I make predictions in an unpredictable life?

Not from Lance, but from the Heart of his Soul,

Your Child,

Lance

Chapter 19

"Scriptures of the Streets"

"Scriptures of the Streets"

Even when you're fed up, always keep your head up,

Soon as you set it down that's when Satan will try to set you up.

Crooked cops, criminals, and killers with the eyes of a hawk,

The block is hot.... You can fry an egg on the sidewalk.

Demons creep trying to pull you six feet deep,

Before you go to sleep, pray to the Lord your soul to keep.

I'm not telling you how to live your life, or how your long story goes,

But if you want to sell drugs I just want to let you know.

My homies died for being dumb, you know the streets never shush,

When a gun is at your temple there's no beating around the bush.

Knowledge is power; the powerless will forever struggle for nothing,

Tell them practice what they preach before they try to come and teach me something.

These are the words that my conscience told me,

Keep your eyes open, and listen to me closely.

Keep a weapon in your reach, and keep your finger on the trigger,

Because the same thing that made you can be the same thing to kill you.

Scriptures of the Streets

March 9, 2013

Dear Dad,

Hey Dad, it's your son Lance. I found out a couple of people I went to middle school with were recently killed execution style. I haven't seen them in forever, so I really didn't know how to feel about the situation. My cousin told me that they were known to live a life of crime, and their previous acts included murder. I was told that they've shot and killed people before. It's so weird how you grow up with someone as a kid, and a decade later they're dead because someone was seeking revenge on them. In these days and time people tend to kill each other for no reason; it's a new style this generation loves to wear. One of my old friends was killed just sitting in his car, and the other was killed over a drug deal gone wrong. I can't even imagine how their parents feel, and the reasons why weren't even worth it. It's like whatever you do as of right now will dictate where you'll be in the future. You know Dad, life is like a game of chess, if you don't have a reason for every move you make, you'll be easy to take out. The same thing that makes you can be the same thing that kills you, so choose the right decisions and never regret anything. I look further down the road so I can have a glimpse of what the destination of a situation may be. I'm not trying to have an early grave, because I have many tasks to complete here on earth. Although I didn't ask to be here, I still strive to become the best person I can be. It's natural that I'm going to make mistakes though, for I'm only human. If more people tried to make an attempt to read the Bible, then there wouldn't be so much madness. Or maybe a translation of the Bible made specifically for the streets would help for a better understanding. Dad, it's like if you don't have a gun then you have no protection, and I hate it with a passion. A gun is nothing but the devil's toy, and the earth is his playground. You have to carry weapons because these idiots can easily get a hold of one as well, and there's no telling what they might decide to do. I pray and stay strong in faith, but why must there be so much evil among us? I feel like evil is here to lure us away from what we were sent here to do, and from the looks of things, the devil is a smooth operator. You can get killed doing what you do for a living, so choose your path wisely; because it'll boomerang back to you in the future. My experiences from life and what I learn outside of home helped mold me to become the person I am today. I never try to sin on purpose, I just do what I have to so I can stay alive and protect my family. Experiences are like scriptures, they helped guide me, and now I know the outcome for many more things. I'm going to continue to learn these scriptures of the streets until the day I die. I pray my death won't be due to my own ignorance, for I'm wiser today than I was yesterday.

Not from Lance, but from the Heart of his Soul,

Your Child,

Lance

Chapter 20
"Keys to Success"

"Keys to Success"

I'm spirited away with the Midas touch, when I turn your life to gold don't get out of control,

This is a gift to you; Not from Lance, but from the heart of his soul.

I couldn't open the door to success, somebody locked it, I don't have the keys, or none of the copies.

So I lace up my timberland boots, when I kick the door down off the hinge just be ready to shoot.

Let's do this for the people with a dream; with no track shoes to chase it or deep breaths to pace it.

Let's do this for the people with a blueprint; with a vision in their head, but no equipment to make it.

Let's do this for the people with a voice; who want to speak up, but have no microphone to record it.

Let's do it for the ones who want to go to college; Dust bunnies live in their pockets so there's no money to afford it.

Let's do this for the people who fought so we could be equal, and please have mercy on my sins because the serpents so lethal,

It injects thoughts saying I can't believe like an atheist, and it left bite marks by my Jesus Christ necklace.

They're reckless, and crashed into my emotions; struck a match, dropped it, and created an explosion.

Don't fight fire with fire because it upgrades to hell, they burned my ancestors alive so cremate me while I'm breathing.

The world spins like an ice ball and it does get colder, people breathing down my neck trying to peep over my shoulder.

First I pause, then I close my eyes,

Praying my poetry is permanent to pass the test of time.

I pray to the Lord that my soul's not erased,

I pull that black ski mask down over my black face.

Draw a cross on my chest; wrap my heart up in a bulletproof vest,

And pray to GOD I don't die stealing the keys to success,

Let's do this for the people with a dream.

Keys to Success

April 13, 2013

Dear Dad,

Hey Dad, It's been harder than ever trying to keep the bills paid and our stomachs full. Auntie Lene was the one who would always provide everything for us, but now that she's gone we have to step up to the plate with a purpose. I can feel her watching over me when I write throughout the night, and I'm going to be the water that hydrates my family tree's roots. Before I left the hospital the night before she passed, I promised her that I was going to take care of the family and keep us molded in good shape, for her blood is my blood. I'm going to be graduating from high school this year, and I've been thinking about all the things I want to do afterwards. Of course I'm going to attend college, but I've been thinking about how I can use my talents to make some income in the process. I've came to the conclusion that you need money to make money, and breaking the broke cycle isn't going to be an easy task. The hardest part of anything is getting started, because you're limited to the options of what you want to do. Life is already hard, but it's even harder when you're a member of the hopeless. You could have a million different ideas in your mind, but reality will lessen the number, because you have to use what you got to get what you want. And when you grow up in the ghetto, the projects don't provide much for you, other than corruption and the ambition to make it out like a soldier at war. Growing up without a father figure to guide me, you could say there is a lot of knowledge that I may not have possessed yet. It's hard trying to pay for your dream when you only have a dollar to your name. I have so much knowledge to spread throughout the world, and I know that my words can help people make it through their hardships. Dad, I promise that I can change the world with the thoughts inside my mind. You hear about all the madness going on in the world, and how more people are committing suicide every day due to lack of spiritual strength, and I feel like I'm sitting on the antidote that can cure the ills of this sick world. But still, the majority of the world doesn't know that I exist. Hope, plus a heart made to love hard; No one knows that I exist. If I were to meet the owner of a major company, I wouldn't have to say much for them to be willing to work with me. They would automatically know right off the bat that I'm aiming for the skies when I step up to the plate. Dad, I'm so passionate about my work, I even start to cry while I'm writing sometimes. I know that I can touch other hearts if I reach out with mine.... but still I have to snap back to reality, because the devil doesn't want me to save the souls of millions. I can see the world through my window, but I can't make my way outside. I can see everything through my window that I would change, but still I'm locked inside without anyone around to free me from my past. I'm blocked by the door because I haven't found the keys to unlock it. As soon as I have the keys to success in my possession, I will be able to go to the rescue for all the pain I saw through my window pane. I feel like the super hero for my generation, and regardless of if I die trying, I'm going to take the keys to success so the people following in my footsteps won't have to struggle as hard. I thank GOD for a chance to change the world, but I cannot waste time celebrating. For I have multiple objectives to complete on my mission; and I don't know if I'll be here tomorrow, so I do all I can to save someone today.

Not from Lance, but from the Heart of his Soul,

Your Child,

Lance

Chapter 21
"Never Been Happy"

"Never Been Happy"

You can watch me like a sniper and still know nothing about me,

Go through high school with me and still know nothing about me.

You can attend church every Sunday; see me in a suit every Sunday,

Have an assigned seat right beside me and still know nothing about me.

Is it the gun, or is it GOD who's my protection?

I'm starting to notice a stranger in my own reflection.

Before my weary eyes I can recognize the deceitful lies,

Internally weeping; my spirit counts all of my tears inside.

Tears took the place of the rain on my window pane,

But there's no doctor in my house to come and cure this type of pain.

I fell toward hell, but His angels were there to catch me,

Until I gave my life to Christ, I've never been happy.

Never Been Happy

May 12, 2013

Dear Dad,

Hey Dad, I finally found the keys to success! They were located in the church the whole time. Today was the day I got baptized. Although I didn't physically see you in attendance, I still felt you in my presence. My cousin gave her life to Christ alongside me, so I didn't go into the water alone. We had been thinking about getting baptized for the longest, but we were just nervous at the time. When we walked to the front of the church to be candidates for baptism, I couldn't do anything but cry the whole time. I didn't even know why I was crying; I had the same warm feeling in my chest that I got before my performances. When I first stepped foot into the water, I felt like I was dehydrated. I probably should've stepped foot in the water a long time ago. If I was to wait any longer than I did, then my soul would've probably died from dehydration. I submerged under the water, but I didn't feel a drop touch my skin. When I stepped out of the water, it was then that I could feel it dripping off my body. I'm happy we decided to get baptized and didn't continue to wait. Tomorrow is on a fool's calendar; you can only live right now. The renaissance of my soul was the turning point of my life. I now know that I'm here for a more specific reason, and there are more tasks to accomplish from the headquarters in Heaven. After I was baptized, I took a deep breath of freedom. My family was happy to see that we were making the right choices in our lives. When we went home, we celebrated with a great Sunday evening feast. Grandma Mozell told me that she knew Auntie Lene was proud of us. Maybe I can be more in tune with my spirit since I now have a clean slate. Before being baptized, I was antisocial everywhere I went, but now I know that a simple smile can make someone's day. The water was like a car wash for my soul, so now

I can see clearly down the road. I still have to be careful because I feel like I'm traveling in uncharted territory. I've never had this feeling before, nor have I been in this state of mind. I continue to pray every day and night, it's like if I forget to pray then I miss my objective for that day. I'm not of this world, and being a baptized enhanced me to become more ambitious of completing my task. I used to never flash a smile, but now I smile to help others; Jesus carried me through the water, now it's my turn to carry someone else. Now there's a difference between not knowing and knowing better; if you continue to disobey when you know better then you're taking a high risk. You risk losing the talents you were blessed with. If you can't handle your gift in a mature manner, then GOD has the power to bless someone else. It's possible to lose your talents due to your own immaturity. I try my best to dodge the devils' temptations; however, I'll never know if I'm about to be blindsided from another angle. Dad, how can I know if Satan's fangs are about to strike?

Not from Lance, but from the Heart of his Soul,

Your Child,

Lance

Chapter 22

"Smoking on Suicide"

"Smoking on Suicide"

I'm an animal without a stimuli, so I hit my knees and pray,

Pray for exposure to my senses without becoming others prey.

Did I die? I'm swallowed by darkness locked inside a black hearse,

When you can no longer control something, you prepare yourself for the worst.

It's a very thin line between not knowing and knowing better,

Ignorance is bliss when born again, but you're no stranger to this weather.

I'm giving my lungs the Black Death every time I take a deep breath,

Inhale the chlorophyll like a breath of fresh air, then exhale a ghost when I blow,

Yes; I'm committing suicide I know.

Smoking on Suicide

May 13, 2013

Dear Dad,

Hey Dad, It's your son Lance. I feel so awful at the moment, and I'm highly disappointed in myself. I got high for the very first time, and now I can't control the thoughts running wild in my head. I made the wrong decision when I was invited to hang out with some people from school. They picked me up and we went to their house. Everything was going great, until someone brought out a gravity bong filled with ice and water. They tried to persuade me to take a hit, but I told them I wasn't a stoner. Everybody else started smoking from the gravity bong and blowing the smoke in my direction. It was so much smoke in the air that it looked like a cloud floated into the room. I don't remember smoking anything, but the last thing I remember was seeing everybody disappear into the cloud like a smoke bomb. I thought I didn't smoke anything, but people were saying they caught me on camera getting high as a kite. I hate this feeling with a passion. I don't even remember what it was that I smoked, it's like my brain went completely blank of everything. The last thing that I remember was Grandma Mozell calling me to see if I was alright. I told her I was fine, and then I got off the phone. It crept me out because she called me right back after I got off of the phone. When I answered her call she asked me, "What's wrong with you, and why are you talking so slow?" To try and avoid her knowing my mistake, I told her I was sleepy so I could get off the phone before she could figure me out. I tried to do everything to get that stuff out my head, and nothing seemed to work. I even tried standing outside half-dressed in the cold, and even that didn't help. I was told that cold water and cool air would make the high fade away, but I guess it doesn't work for me. I was so messed up that I started to see nude demons running around me. I knew it was just my hot air balloon brain playing tricks on me, or at least I hope. Control, control, control. Being in control of your actions is the most important thing you can do. If there comes a time when you can't control your own actions, then you're in jeopardy. From this day forward I refuse to let anything have control over me again, because I have too much at stake to not be in control of my actions. I was told I would be able to write for days in this state of mind, but I couldn't write a single word! I've learned another scripture of the street from my mistake. I feel like I'm killing myself on purpose. If I continue to bury myself alive under the wrong decisions, then my health will start to descend. If my family needed me right now, I wouldn't be able to come to their rescue. Please forgive me for my sinful ways. I just got baptized yesterday, and now I'm trapped in the devils' closet. How did I get here? I pray that I'm protected while in this vulnerable stage, because I feel like an animal without a stimuli. Dad, how am I supposed to survive when I'm incarcerated by bad decisions?

Not from Lance, but from the Heart of his Soul,

Your Child,

Lance

Chapter 23
"Disobedience"

"Disobedience"

Forgive them, for they have bitten from the forbidden fruit,

The apple juice dripping from their chin was the proof....

You had borders set up, but still I chose to jump the fence,

I didn't follow instructions; so I died due to disobedience.

At night as I lie on my pillow my thoughts huddle up and ponder,

Sketching up plans to find answers to my wonders.

I sinned worse than Adam and Eve, and I was exiled none;

Does this make my existence a conundrum?

I took a bath in Holy water so my soul would be cleansed,

I inhaled a scent of sin; and like a filthy pig I got dirty again.

I too am guilty of stabbing my teeth in the heart of the forbidden fruit,

For the apple juice dripping from my chin is the proof....

Disobedience

May 16, 2013

Dear Dad,

I've been high for the past three days from that one night! I don't understand why my decisions started to get harder soon as I was baptized. It's like there's a million different routes at the forks in the road; and my last decision ate me up like I was the main dish on the devils dinner table. Does this mean the devil is sending reinforcements to try and bring me down? I've never had so many decisions come across me at one time. It feels like Satan knows that I'm a soldier of GOD now, so his snipers will be watching my every move from this point forward. I know I'm guilty of disobedience, and I haven't even been judged yet. This must be the feeling that Adam and Eve experienced at the beginning of time. Ignorance is bliss when you're a child, so did the renaissance of my soul make me a child again spiritually? Or did it test my instincts to see if I was really ready for the world? I now have no choice but to be ready, because the devil has already damaged me with bad decisions. My baptism was a symbol of sacrifice, and I agreed to leave my past life behind me. It was like a contract, and my soul signed the dotted line in the blood of Jesus Christ. Dad, I ask for forgiveness for my sins, for I'm only human. Not everyone on earth is going to be a perfect little angel. I once traveled to the Garden of Eden and bitten from the forbidden fruit. Adam and Eve were exiled for sinning one time, so it scares me thinking about the consequences for how much we sin today. I'm ashamed of myself for sinning the very next day after my baptism. I've never been the type of person to try drugs, not even for the fun of it. I still don't regret anything I've done, because it was a lesson to be learned. Life is a sequence of struggles and a pattern of problems; and you never understand things until you experience them first hand. My uncle told me that life was going to get harder after my baptism, because we live in sin where horns are hidden in everyone's reflection. Dad, it's like you can tell a child not to do something, but they'll still disobey so they can have the learning experience. A child can disobey his father and learn from his mistake; but in my case the teacher never showed up for class. I know I was wrong, and from Heavens eyes they were probably disgusted with my actions. I ask for forgiveness from my downfall of deceit. I now have the learning experience of how the devil's going to try and persuade me more than ever. Satan's going to try and point me in a direction that's going to take me on a detour from my destination in Heaven. Hopefully, the other side of the golden gates will be my final destination. I pray for discipline and direction to guide me through the wilderness of life. I'm on the lookout for devils in the distance and serpents slithering beneath my feet. You never know what will cross your path as you walk alone in this world; because the devil has the ability to become camouflage with the things your heart desires.

Not from Lance, but from the Heart of his Soul,

Your Child,

Lance

Chapter 24

"The Devil's Cigar"

"The Devil's Cigar"

The devil wants me in handcuffs and incarcerated behind bars,

I'm playing dodge ball with the fireballs at the end of his cigar.

We all make mistakes so we take one step at a time,

What would you do if you could rewind back time?

My friends claimed to be trustworthy, then they tried to grab me,

They only had my back so they could turn around and stab me.

The devil has a job, and I refuse to let him crush me,

I'm being held in the palms of the Lords hands, so Lucifer cannot touch me.

I'm God's son; from my head to my toes and all throughout my soul,

I'm 100 percent Harvest with that harvester of sorrows.

Don't trade dialogue with the cops, they'll pick you and flick you,

And when they put you in the system.... They might forget you.

We're getting smoked away because we're living so far,

It's like we're living at the end of the devil's cigar.

Don't let the fire burn you, because every single day,

People are blowing in the wind,

Getting smoked away.

The Devil's Cigar

May 20, 2013

Dear Dad,

Hey Dad, you won't believe how the devil tried to get me burned this time. One of my old friends from school asked me to hang out with him. I went not knowing what he really had planned. I dressed in new clothes because I was told we were going to the mall and to see a movie. When he got to my house, I got in the back seat because another companion of his was in the passenger's seat. I noticed after a while that we weren't headed in the direction of the mall, nor the movies. They drove all the way to the back of a subdivision till the pavement turned into a dirt road. I asked where we were going, but no one said a word or looked in my direction. I saw the headlights point out another car parked in the distance, and when we got closer they cut their headlights off. My fake friends got out the car and went to the other one that was parked. I didn't know where I was, so I didn't move a muscle. They got back out, and the other car quickly sped past my window. When my fake friends returned, they pulled out handfuls of marijuana and started lighting it inside the car. I was guilty of this same crap right after I was baptized, and now the devil's trying to force it into my lungs. I was so provoked that I got out the car and started walking away. I called Valerie to tell her what happened and she was worried about me, because neither of us knew where I was. Time sprinted by quickly, and my phones battery died. I had no communication device, I was stranded in the middle of nowhere, and I was surrounded by a bunch of cannabis! I can't even trust the people I grew up with. All of my friends have officially downgraded to associates. Friends are a figment of my imagination. I'd rather walk alone barefoot on concrete, than to walk on a thin line with a group of people I don't need. Before my phone died; I scrolled through my contacts and deleted everybody I didn't need to succeed in life, and over half of my contacts were gone. I refuse to let someone contaminate my success because they can't get their life together. I had to circumcise those people out of my life. It's not me being selfish, it's just me being smart. I got back into the car and demanded to go home. Soon as I closed the door I saw blue and red lights flashing through the trees…. Soon as the cops came around the corner; the dummies in my car decided to speed off, hoping it would take the cruiser time to turn back around. Now I'm in the car with pounds of marijuana that has nothing to do with me, and we're speeding through a subdivision trying to out run a police cruiser. If we get caught; then I'm going to jail just for being in the car, and everything I have going for me will be flushed down the drain. We were able to dodge the cops, and they lost sight of us in a crowded restaurant parking lot. We watched them pass us by and continue down the road. I told them to take the back roads and return me to my home. Those were the only words I said to them for the rest of the night. Dad, it felt like I was a piece of weed rolled up in the devil's cigar, and he put it out right before he was about to inhale me. I was right there at the end of his bud, but I was happy to be a roach that night. Lucifer will use people close to you to lure you into the shell of his cigar. Then when he sets you on fire you have nowhere to go but through his black lips, and into the air with the rest of the smoked souls. I found out who the people in the other car were. One of them got shot in the head and the other got arrested. I could've easily been in the same predicaments, but I thank GOD I wasn't one of the people blowing in the wind from the devil's cigar. Dad, how will I know who to trust when my closest friends are devils in disguises?

Not from Lance, but from the Heart of his Soul,

Your Child,

Lance

Chapter 25
"Farewell"

"Farewell"

I say my farewell to this foster life I was forced to live,

The depths of the projects were my orphanage.

I put those angel wings on my back like a jet pack,

And fire them up like a rocket ship because I'm on my way.

I exhaled a ghost, and just like my soul it evaporates,

Will my name be on the guest list at the golden gates?

At the Heaven Hotel, will I have a halo to stay in town?

Or thumb a taxi to ride the highway to hell back down?

No turkey on Thanksgiving, but still I love my mother,

We went from no food in the fridge to having a feast like the Last Supper.

In my prince of Egypt robe, I'm showered in gold; welcome to my palace,

I hold out my gold pinky ring when I take mini sips from my gold chalice.

The diamond crown matches the diamond ring, and everybody claims that I changed,

But every time I glance in the mirror my identical twin still looks the same.

Mirror, mirror on the wall; who's the most ambitious of them all?

When you reach these heights, people think the world's in your hands like a stress ball.

But it's on your shoulders like a wounded soldier, and it's hard to carry,

I keep my mouth closed like a virgins legs, and if I do speak a blessing is born like the Virgin Mary.

Lucifer fell from Heaven, but I didn't wish upon his star,

So you don't have to shed no tears when you see those bullet holes in my car.

I got shot by a shooting star, and baptized in a wishing well,

My dreams will take me far, so I say my farewell.

Farewell

May 24, 2013

Dear Dad,

Hey Dad, guess who just graduated from high school. It was another rare time when I felt you in my presence without seeing you. I'm so happy I'm done with that school and all the childish people in it. I'm looking forward to bigger and better things, never to look back. I almost didn't make it to graduation because everybody was playing around at the house, but I was there and that's all that matters. I also won scholarships and awards for college, so I was in a good position. Graduation was the beginning of my new life, and I had a better view on the world. I left behind a lot of people who I thought I could trust, and I can barely see them in my rearview mirror. My old life is behind me and I'm running away from it as far as possible. High school was only a learning process, but the hardest test doesn't end here. It's all about the things you do after graduation that determines who you really are. I know that I'm going to attend college and try to make some income with my talents. As long as you have that diploma with your name printed on it, you have proof that says you've served your time. It's crazy how a piece of paper runs the physical world. When I put on my cap and gown, I felt like a super hero putting on his cape. I was confident that there was nothing in this world that I couldn't accomplish. The world belonged to me when the bell rung on the last day of school. There is nothing that can stop me from being all I'm meant to be. When my name was called at graduation, I felt the same warm feeling in my chest. The stage felt like a wobbly bridge when I started walking, and I didn't look back for no one. When my diploma was placed in my hand, it felt like I was being given the world on a golden platter. I'm older and my decisions will dictate my life from this point forward. I didn't go to any graduation parties, because I wasn't going to look at people if I didn't have to. I looked at the Class of 2013 over half of my life, so why would I want to see them after graduation. I will not be found when they come looking for me because I'll be living in my dreams. I'm moving out the house to go live in the moment. I've served my time and now I have my ticket that says I'm free to go. Instead of crying and waving goodbye, I shot them a bird like I was hunting quail. I have the passport to my dreams in my possession. As I step on the plane, I say farewell to the old life that I used to live, along with the fake people in it. And even if my flight doesn't make it, my angel wings will fly me even further.... I'm going to make it or die trying. My old life is a fossil, so now is the time to fulfill my purpose. I'm saying farewell to my old life because my younger variation is dead. Dad, does the distance between us make it seem like I'm dead to you?

Not from Lance, but from the Heart of his Soul,

Your Child,

Lance

Chapter 26
"Grape Garden"

"Grape Garden"

They don't want us to succeed,

They don't want to water us, and watch us grow up from a seed.

They'd rather chop us down, and watch us fall,

Like Jack and the Beanstalk when we make it to the top,

They want to chop us down like trees, I heard somebody scream timber,

These wood peckers knock on wood so much that they can't feel the splinters.

Because they're numb to the pain, I bow my head and try not to panic,

Even on a good day in the sunlight we got hung like hammocks.

So they could lie on their backs and relax, it was illegal to be Black in this town,

And the dress code didn't include a cap and gown.

So I sent prayers to the post office in Heaven;

Angel wings are the flight to my foreign dreams,

So why am I having flashbacks of 9/11?

Because they don't want me to possess the power,

So they gave us plane tickets, and reserved seats on the twin towers.

Just to kill us all and watch us fall, in the dark I couldn't see,

Hold onto my hand tight as you can so you're not lost in the cloud of debris.

It was hard to breathe; they asked why loose limbs were lying at
the murder scene,

They amputated my friendship, and cut me off like the guillotine.

Blood spilled, and they watched my head roll down the hill like
Jack and Jill,

In my tumbled thoughts I know they're greedy for the greed,

Because they don't want us to succeed.

They don't want to water us, and watch us grow up from a seed.

They'd rather chop us down, and watch us fall,

Like Jack and the Beanstalk when we make it to the top,

They want to chop us down, I'm free falling baby,

Waiting for an angel to swoop down and save me.

You say life is hard; well I beg your pardon,

It's harder when you're planted and raised in the grape garden.

Grape Garden

August 16, 2013

Dear Dad,

Hey Dad, reality has been trying to knock me out cold since graduation. I feel like I'm tied down to train tracks; that's how hard reality hit me! You don't get a taste of real life until after you graduate. You have to go back to the drawing board and create a new blueprint for your new environment; that's if you want to adapt to the real world. Being black in America only amplifies the difficulty of succeeding in this world. Dad, I love every race on the face of this earth, but that's not how everyone sees it. Alabama's largest city Birmingham was once known as Bombingham. The racial wars were bloodier than the battle of Antietam, and most African Americans didn't even fight back. Still to this day, I notice racism in our society; and my ancestors died over equality. Slavery ended over a century ago, so why is the color of my skin still an issue? It's hard growing up without a father regardless of what race you are, but it's even harder when you have a dark history hidden in your heritage. People assume the taste of dark colored fruit won't be satisfying to their taste buds, but they must remember that the darkest fruits are the sweetest of them all. Dad, I sometimes feel like a grape that sprouted in the moonlight, but no one wants to see me grow. They fear what I'll become, so they chop me down for their entertainment. They watch us fall like the World Trade Center, and no one searches ground zero for any survivors; so I had to find my own way out. I've lacked guidance my whole life and I've made it this far. Going against the grain of all odds is nothing new to me. I mapped out a blueprint that would put me where I want to be, but still I can only take one step at a time. If I try to take too many steps at once, then I'm going to fall into another bad decision. Reality wants me to take one step forward and two steps back. I bloomed in the grape vines, and we were surrounded by thorns like barbed wire. I wasn't properly watered because they didn't want me to grow. The pain caused so much precipitation from my eyelids, so I wept an ocean and watered myself. The roots of my soul grew into a vine that would hydrate my family tree for generations to come. I've tried my best, I've gone against all odds, and I've failed numerous times. I've returned to my feet in search for the next opportunity, because I refuse to become a statistic. The fallen angel forgot to cut down the last grape vine in the garden, because I bloomed into his worst nightmare.... Success with a Negro presence; yes we exist!

Not from Lance, but from the Heart of his Soul,

Your Child,

Lance

Chapter 27

"Drowning in Your Dreams"

"Drowning in Your Dreams"

Last night I went to sleep with my headphones on my head,

Music was playing against the pillow beating bass through the bed.

Music notes floated from my ears into a highway of rhythm,

One of the most beautiful things I've ever seen; is this the pathway to my dreams?

As I started walking, a strange, but familiar voice started talking,

"I was headed to the store and I wanted to take you,

You were dozed off catching Z's so I didn't want to wake you,

I heard the records you recorded and might I say I loved them so,

If the lights poof off while you're performing,

You would still put on a show,

Express yourself with your wealth and sell some gold records for me.

Pay no attention to the stop signs once you've spotted your dreams,

Combine your soul with your passion and no one can come between,

I will always love you like the beautiful bright star that you are."

Drowning in Your Dreams

September 23, 2013

Dear Dad,

Hey Dad, I have some amazing news to share with you! I previously signed up for a production program, and we work on stuff I actually want to learn. The first day we were interviewed on our visions in life, and we had to write one word that described us on a big sheet of paper. My word was AMBITIOUS, and I taped it to my ceiling so I would see it every morning when I wake up. My work ethic is ambitious because I know how it feels to have my creativity caged by circumstances. It's not my fault that I had to endure more than the average adolescent, but it will be my fault if I let my circumstances come in the way of my dreams. Dreams visit me in my sleep, but the process of bringing them into reality doesn't come overnight. I've been writing my whole life, but still I have to practice patient. Patience gives your dream peace at mind, and allows it time to grow into what you want. While I'm diving into my writing, I must remember that creativity is only half of the process, because the business side is equal in importance. It's important to protect your intellectual property, because there are snakes in suits that'll try to take advantage of you. It's not easy noticing these serpents slithering around your intellectual property; because just like Lucifer, these snakes have the ability to become camouflage with the things you love and desire. These serpents will present themselves as if they can make your dreams come true, but in reality they're merely trying to claim something they didn't create. These serpents in the shadows can cause your brightest dreams to transform into your darkest nightmares.

Dad, I've had an encounter with a snake in a suit, and it took me years to notice his fangs that were injecting lies into my life. I thought I could trust this encounter who seemed to care for my dream, but I felt like I wasn't taking advantage of the time that was passing me by. Disagreements started to take place more often, because I realized that his true intentions were not to help me, but to use me to benefit himself. I felt like a caged bird; because I had the wings to fly away, but I didn't have enough space to sprint and take flight. I was anchored by limitations, but when I slayed this serpent in the shadow I shattered all shackles and broke free. I realized that the only person I needed was the man in the mirror, and after cutting the serpent out of my life I was able to fly at my desired heights.

The only person who was required to believe in my dream was myself, and I started to notice a difference in my networking skills. Something told me to prepare myself, because my jigsaw puzzle was finally coming together. The thought of it made me feel like I could finally pursue my purpose, and share my work with the world. I informed Mother on my recent encounter with the snake in a suit. I was alright for the first couple of minutes, and then I felt the same warm feeling in my chest.... And out of nowhere tears started racing down my cheeks. I had no idea why I was crying, but then I realized the possibilities of what had just happened. I knew soon I would be able to bless my Mother with what she deserves, because I could finally fly at my full potential. I know how it feels to have a million ideas incarcerated inside your skull without a way to reveal them to the world. I almost drowned in the possibilities of where I could go; that's if I stay focus and keep my head on straight. I noticed the possibilities were all of my dreams; and I jumped into the pool of possibilities head first. My mind is full of creative ideas, and I'm going to spread them throughout the world like wildfire. The encounter with the serpent was a turning point in my career, and ever since then I've had a sharper perspective on every business decision that came my way. I knew the sooner I started working, the sooner I would be where I wanted in life. Dad, don't throw me a life jacket or safe rings, because I'm going to drown in my dreams.

Not from Lance, but from the Heart of his Soul,

Your Child,

Lance

Chapter 28
"I Don't Understand"

"I Don't Understand"

I don't understand why countries have wars,

Soldiers coming home covered in sores.

I don't understand why life is designed for us to die,

We shed thick salty tears,

But no one cares why.

I don't understand the hatred pointed towards my pigment,

I'm incarcerated by hate, locked away from my innocence.

I don't understand why soldiers put their lives on the line,

Do they sacrifice their life so I can live out mine?

I don't know.

But what I do understand is that GOD stays above them,

Not knowing what's going to happen on the battlefield,

But knowing GOD will always love them.

I Don't Understand

October 12, 2013

Dear Dad,

Hey Dad, everyone at church loves to hear what I write about, and I even had a request for a specific piece. I'm a member of a mentoring group called From Boys to Men. During the meetings, we learn something new about life. Sometimes we have a guest speaker come and speak about their success story. Occasionally we go on field trips to historic landmarks and learn more in depth about our history. The Boys to Men program is inspired by the famous Frederick Douglass quote, "It is [much] easier to build strong children than to repair broken men." The older people in the program help teach the youth how to mature from boys to men. It's a wonderful sight to see young children being guided in the right direction. One of the teachers was retiring from the military, and he was having a retirement ceremony to celebrate his time of duty. He asked me if I could come up with something to say at his ceremony. I brainstormed about a soldier's mentality. I never understood why we were at war with each other, so I named the piece, "I Don't Understand." I talked about my perspectives on war, and compared them to how Jesus would want things to be. When I recited the poem at church, I had people in tears on the edge of their seats. The same warm feeling returned to my chest; but I tried to ignore it and remain focused on delivering my message. Not long after the retirement ceremony, I found out my great granddaddy passed away, yet alone I didn't even know he was still living! You can't know about your roots if your father's not there to inform you.

My great granddaddy (Melvin Ballard) was a true war hero.... I found out that he was a World War II Veteran! After reciting my poem, "I Don't Understand," it felt like I was trying to give myself a heads up about the situation. I was so upset that I didn't know what to do. If I knew he was still living, I would've had so much to talk to him about. There are conversations that'll never take place, and there are stories that'll never be told. He survived the war and was awarded the highest civilian honor, the Congressional Gold Medal Award. He was one of the first black Montfort Point Marines. It provokes me to find out this information from the newspaper, and not from my own father!!! I attended his funeral, and the whole time I heard my poem replay over and over again in the back of my head. At the gravesite, the Marines fired their rifles into the air before they buried my great grandfather. And my brain fired the same poem in my skull as he was lowered into the ground. The further he went, the closer I got to the end of the poem in my head; and it ended exactly when he was six feet deep.... I don't understand this war, I don't understand this world, and I don't understand why a father wouldn't nurture his seed to enrich its growth.

Not from Lance, but from the Heart of his Soul,

Your Child,

Lance

Chapter 29
"The Brightest Smile"

"The Brightest Smile"

My imagination can't imagine, and my imagination can't believe,

You watched me come into this world and I had to watch you leave.

This isn't a fairy tale, so who is Cinderella?

Pain follows me around like a rain cloud is my umbrella.

I feel possessed with a thousand pounds of stress on my chest,

I can only handle so much; I let GOD bench press the rest.

Regardless how hard I try, the words I write will never explain,

The invisible war that's steady going on in my brain.

The fork in the road separates the wrongs from the rights,

You can't fight something that was planned when GOD made light.

Rest in peace, and live happily in harmony,

Tell GOD I said hello and kiss a prayer for me.

There are warm colors on the color wheel when you're feeling down and blue,

Heaven is my home; so when you see me, I'm just passing through....

Steady passing through the rain,

My good days outweigh my bad days,

So I will never complain.

I apologize for the hypnotized whom takes a vision for granted,

GOD has always had a plan even though I'll never understand it.

His ways are not my ways, and His thoughts are not my thoughts,

But I know He knows what's best for me so I don't even talk,

I just smile.

The Brightest Smile

November 12, 2013

Dear Dad,

Hey Dad, I turned nineteen years old two days ago. I didn't feel like doing much; so we had cake and ice cream, and Valerie came over to spend time with me. I'm blessed to have made it this far, because I could've been dead or in jail just like my peers in the devils cigar. My old high school principal was going through some hardships, because his mom passed away. I was thinking about how I could help him get through his time of need. I came to the conclusion that I could do something similar to what I did for Valerie's mom. I tried to come up with a concept that would make him smile afterwards, so I named it "The Brightest Smile." I drew angels smiling and flying around the poem, and then topped it all off with a rose boarder. I've always tried my best to help people in any way I could, and it felt like a job that was more relevant than a nine to five. I'd rather make a living doing what I love other than settling for a job that wasn't destined for me. When I do a specific piece for someone, I try to go deep as the ocean floor. People feel like it's specifically for their pain because that's how I programed the words. It was a cold rainy morning, and the sun was playing hide and go seek with the clouds. I brought the poster for my former principal to my old high school, and the lady at the front desk gazed at it in amazement. She clenched her chest after reading the poem, and she said the poster was going to make him smile. When my former principal was done with his morning meeting, he told me to step into his office. I handed him the poster without saying a word; just to see his reaction. I saw his eyes start to water as he observed the piece. After he read the poem, he turned around and hugged me so tight that I could barely breathe. He told me how thankful he was to have me do something like that for him. Then he told me to get out his office so I wouldn't see him cry. Before I left he told me that I turned his day upside down and gave him something to smile for.

The heartfelt moment made me think about Valerie. She lost her mother as well, and was melancholy with a low self-esteem. She rarely spoke to anyone, but now she's always smiling and brightening everyone's day. She's a freshmen in college now, and she's going to major in Business. She's the complete opposite from the girl I met at the dance. The girl at the dance had a low self-esteem, and was clueless of her purpose in life. After she lost her mother, she lost herself in the world. Valerie was forced to mature without her mother's guidance into adulthood. She didn't have a role model who'd fulfill her mother's duties, so she was forced to walk into uncharted territory. She could've easily given up; but she continued to search inside her heart until she figured herself out. She wants to show her mom that she's capable of reaching her dreams. People doubted her all throughout her childhood, and she has proven them wrong by simply being herself. She made mistakes along the way, but she eventually matured. She reminds me of myself, because we both overcame our childhood challenges without both parents in attendance. I'm in love with Valerie, and I'm proud to see the strong woman she has become. I know her mother is proud, because I see a golden glow in the dimples of her smile. Valerie overcame her childhood challenges, so now she must overcome her adulthood difficulties. I know how it feels to walk alone in this world; because without a dad in my life, it was the only way I knew how to travel.

Not from Lance, but from the Heart of his Soul,

Your Child,

Lance

Chapter 30
"Photographic Memories"

"Photographic Memories"

Memories are a way of holding onto the moments you love and treasure,

Collect them and store them in your heart, for they will last forever.

There are so many that I had to keep fond,

For all my loved ones blowing in the wind gone.

Now you're in Heaven looking down upon me,

When you flew away, your memories constantly rained down upon me.

I never had the chance to tell you goodbye,

The only thing I can do is break down and cry.

And I'm left swimming in my tears of deceit,

Dead broke, but still I refuse to fall from my feet.

Every night when I lie in my bed,

I watch the flashbacks go by like a slide show in my head.

It's all a part of life from the cradle to the grave,

Live a whole lifetime and your soul is to save.

Without a halo you can't get through Heaven's gate,

Hold on to it along with faith, and never let it break.

My family watched me sprout up,

I was a 13 year old teen, but in my head I was grown up.

When I grow up, as a kid what did I say?

Never in their life will my family have to work another day.

Finding someone to love me was never the case,

But still I shed a tear when I glance at your face.

To keep my memories I write songs and I rhyme,

Store them in my heart for they will last a whole lifetime.

There are so many memories ever since I was a child,

But in the end I can still smile,

Gazing at these photographic memories.

Photographic Memories

December 25, 2013

Dear Dad,

Hey Dad, once again another Christmas has gone by, and it was hard for us to get into the spirit this year. When Auntie Lene was living, she was the one who got everybody whatever they wanted on their Christmas list. She was the heartbeat of our family tree, but now it's my responsibility to provide a pulse. Christmas was melancholy without Auntie Lene, and her loss is a tattoo that'll remain on my heart until I see her again. I was going through my dressers, and I came across some photos from last Christmas. Auntie Lene looked so beautiful and happy. I keep her in my heart, so she's always with me everywhere I go. Staring at the photos made me wonder what she was thinking, and is she proud of her nephew? My last words to her was a promise, and I promised her that I was going to take care of our family. I'm going to do everything I can to keep my promise; it's shatterproof, so it will never be broken. I looked at the photos of Auntie Lene while thinking about all the good times we shared. It made me so happy that I forgot she passed away....

I still look for her sometimes; it feels like she's going to walk into the room like she's still here. Dad, they can call me crazy all they want to, because I still have conversations with her. I can't hear what she's saying, but I can feel the meaning of her words inside my heart. It's like seeing the effect before you know the cause. Dad, I miss her so much, and I wonder if she's watching me write you this letter right now. I remember when she would dance and listen to her records all night long. The party was always where Auntie Lene got comfortable. Some nights they would be at the swimming pool, and other nights they would be on her porch with all the puzzles. Wherever they went, you would always hear old school music. Auntie Lene had a record player in her room for when she really wanted to go back into the day. Under the last photo in my dresser I saw her obituary.... And it pulled me out the frame of the photographic memories. I felt the same warm feeling in my chest as I opened it. I couldn't bear to look at my love who helped raise and protect me, and she was always there for me. I feel her in my heart, so she didn't leave me by my lonesome. The cavities of my thoughts crumble till I fall to the floor; I pray until my knees bleed, and this time I almost drowned in my own blood. I depended on Auntie Lene, and her photos reminded me that people were depending on me. I want my photographic memories to be the stitches to close bleeding hearts as well; that's if anyone ever comes across them when I'm gone.

Not from Lance, but from the Heart of his Soul,

Your Child,

Lance

Chapter 31
"Anniversary of a Nightmare"

"Anniversary of a Nightmare"

Last night I had a dream, and it was similar to Martin Luther King's,

We had more gold than the pharaohs, and we were all kings & queens.

All the angels knew their worth, Heaven on earth, it was the perfect place,

Tears were erased, and every juvenile had a smile drawn on their face.

Then the devil sent a dark cloud, when it rained it poured and flooded my fortress,

I found out that the roads to riches were merely crash courses.

It brought an intruder, and he tied a noose tight around my neck,

Then I jumped out my sleep to the ice sickles of a cold sweat....

I had a nightmare Mama, and I didn't know what to do,

Mama you're the light in the darkness, because a halo shines upon you.

I thank you, if it wasn't for you I would've never made it,

Daddy was incarcerated, and clueless of the monster he created.

Mama I thank you, for providing H2O to your unborn seed,

When I sprouted out your flower pot, you watered me and took care of me.

Forsaken by my father, he got ghost and forgot about me,

Now it's like paranormal activity, and he's haunting me.

Anniversary of a Nightmare

January 6, 2014

Dear Dad,

Hey Dad, it has been a year since Auntie Lene's death, and the pain feels no different from a year ago. The pain feels like a tattoo on my soul. I've been having a strange feeling lately, like someone has been watching my every move. Is it another one of Satan's scandalous schemes? I tried to go to sleep, but my suicidal thoughts won't allow me.... Someone once told me the weaker you are, the more you pray, and I've been praying more than ever. I used to pray for my dreams, but now I pray for the strength to overcome my worst nightmares. I have no idea how, but the suicidal thoughts tattooed on my past made their way back into the spotlight. Soon as I think I have everything figured out, I'm pulled back to square one in the blink of an eye. The circumference of my circle of friends has shrunken dramatically, and I no longer associate myself with the devils in disguise. I know I can't trust specific people anymore, regardless if I grew up with them or not. I try writing my suicidal thoughts down on paper; because it's a way I can channel negative energy in a different direction. When I was in elementary school; Dad, believe it or not, but the first poem I ever wrote was a suicide note. When I channel negative energy onto the paper, it's like poison in a bottle. If someone reads it then they'll get the same feeling I had, if not worst. I don't present all my writings to Mother, because some of them are not meant to be heard. Some are only meant to be put on paper, so they won't intoxicate my mind and cause me to do something of the unknown. I didn't understand how to channel negative energy when I was younger, because I tried not to think about it. So when I thought I was sleeping it off, I was really telling those suicidal thoughts to make themselves at home. My mind is an abandoned hotel where suicidal thoughts used to live. I'm glad that I struggled with my emotions earlier, because now I have the upper hand on whatever enters my mind. I'm only human so I'll always pray throughout the day; I can walk alone in this world physically, but not spiritually. That's why I write you so many letters in my times of despair. Whether it's out of happiness or sadness, I'm praying in a puddle of tears until I can swim to a better island. One that will nurture me with my necessities to survive. I'll return home one day, but I'll never know if my room's being reserved for me or not. I pray that it still has my name written on the door.

Not from Lance, but from the Heart of his Soul,

Your Child,

Lance

Chapter 32
"Wet Mail"

"Wet Mail"

Rain falls like my tears and there's no tissue to stop it,

This world that we think is so big is only a speck in GOD's pocket.

What we think are Heavens doors is really His mailbox,

People are mailed to Him every day, so continue to pray.

When I get mailed I hope my nightly prayers never failed,

Place me in peace when decease where we can have a great feast.

Open a chapter that will celebrate the life that is after,

I will live happily ever after when I enter the hereafter.

Jesus delivered me before, and now he's delivering me again,

Not into this world of sin, but where happiness never ends.

In the beginning it felt like we were never winning,

I believe in the Lord because I'm depending on Him to lead me,

I'm leaning on Him to keep me strong as my family leans on me.

You're not closing my casket; you're sealing my letter,

Sending me to an address where it will forever be better.

You're not crying on my casket; you're crying on my letter,

It will still be delivered regardless of the rainy wet weather.

I will never know if I'm delivered to Heaven or Hell,

So I pray until my knees bleed; hoping GOD receives my wet mail.

He unlocks His mailbox.

Wet Mail

March 9, 2014

Dear Dad,

      Hey Dad, it's your son Lance. I wonder where you've been my entire life, and why none of my photographic memories include you in the picture frame. I wonder if you would even cry if I was to die today; or if you would even attempt to come to my funeral. Words can't explain how it feels to have a scotoma where my father was supposed to be. I try to ignore it, but my conscious reminds me with the experiences I learned from. A lot of people who went through the same hardships aren't living today. They're either blowing in the wind; or getting burned in the devils cigar about to join the others in his ash tray. I've learned so much growing up without a father guiding me through life. I accept the man in the mirror, and I wouldn't change one thing if I had to do it all over again. I wouldn't be who I am today if it wasn't for my struggles and mistakes. They're the foundation I stand on when I make a hard life decision, and they point me in a different direction. Once you find your purpose, you are no longer hypnotized by the ills of this sick world; because you've been cured with understanding. By understanding why you walk alone in this world, you have found the path that was designed specifically for you. You now know your purpose, and the distance you must travel to reach your next destination. Your journey might be similar to someone else's, but no two journeys are exactly the same. The wisdom at the end of your journey is worth struggling for, so that's why life is a pattern of painful problems. We're all born into sin and lost without a map, but our struggles place us on the path to the promise land. All we must do is make the right decisions at the forks in the road. I'm thankful that I've learned from my mistakes, and I don't regret any of my failures. Every day without a father was a brick in my life, and over time it built a base for me to stand on; so now I can touch the sky with ease. It feels like the only thing I haven't experienced is death, and my father's absence wouldn't delay my flight. I've written you letters all throughout my life, and I pray that you receive the most important letter of them all; Even if it's wet mail.

Not from Lance, but from the Heart of his Soul,

Your Child,

Lance

Chapter 33

"What Daddy Didn't Know"

"What Daddy Didn't Know"

I was told….

If you don't want to live your life sadly,

Don't follow in the footsteps of your physical daddy.

We're supposed to be close, like a lawyer and his brief case,

Like father like son, but not in this case.

He inhales cannabis like its oxygen, and drinks beer like its
water,

His habits haunted his son and created the worst nightmare.

I didn't have enough muscle to close Pandora's Box,

Now my mind is twisted harder than Bob Marley's dreadlocks.

Out of all the messages you sent me, I read zero love letters,

Your opinion plus your absence doesn't make it any better.

The landlord has us living in a landslide,

We're falling to the depths running out of breath, and there's
nowhere to hide.

In times of danger I had no father figure to call,

I made nineteen birthday wishes, but still didn't receive one call.

Daddy wants to yell at me, and daddy wants to start fussing,

Daddy was never there so daddy couldn't tell me nothing.

Your second chance ran out of time like a bombs countdown….

And you chose to blow it,

I know why you're mad, because you messed up and you know it.

Why does part of it feel like it's my fault? I wonder....

"You weren't an accident," Those are words from my Mother.

Sweet Mother, I will always be by your side,

You've been rolling along down this weary road for too long.

You raised a man by yourself, and I couldn't win for losing,

Mommy; I will always love you like Whitney Houston.

Mama what is it that you saw in my father?

Could it be that you saw me with your Heavenly eyes?

Tragedy would visit more than he did, and even though I can't stand it,

I will still obey the 5th commandment.

What daddy didn't know is that his son was suicidal,

Looking in the mirror staring back at my rival.

I don't feel loved, Honestly, I feel hated,

He only tries to call me when he gets incarcerated.

His maturity level is mediocre, and I understand now,

Why it felt like I was writing letters to another child like a pen pal.

Even though it seems like I'm mad at you all the time,

I never said I didn't love you....

Not even one time.

What Daddy Didn't Know

April 25, 2014

Dear Father,

The journey's been long, but I have an even longer distance to travel in life. I'll never know when the sun's going to set on my timeline. I don't regret any of my falls, because they taught me how to get back up without a helping hand. It provokes me with a passion to not have my physical father in my life, but still I have to rise like Your Son on Easter Sunday. I was once a mistake in the making, but now I'm a hero at work. I'm fighting for everybody in the world who's a victim of the fatherless generation. I'm fighting for the love every father should have for his child. I'm fighting for every single mother who's playing both roles of guardianship. I've watched Mother struggle since the day I was born. I've seen her give her last just so I wouldn't go hungry, and I've seen her raise the boy in the mirror until he became a man. Being a mother is a full-time job, and I know because Mother was by my side regardless of what situation I stumbled into. I could've been incarcerated or six feet deep in an eternal sleep; but Mother made the daily sacrifices to hydrate my roots and enrich my growth. I'm fighting to break the repetition of chains keeping every fatherless child shackled down. I'm fighting for fatherless children so they won't get sucked into the black hole their father was supposed to patch up. I'm fighting for misguided children who still have time to turn their lives around. Statistics have stated that I was destined to fail in life due to my father's absence. I'm not a statistic, because I refuse to be a clone of the failure who planted me. I'm fighting for change in fathers fortunate enough to have their children under the same roof as them. I encourage every fortunate father to remain present in their child's life, because it truly makes a difference in the direction they choose to take. It warms my heart when I see a father with his child in public, because it lets me know that one less kid won't suffer as much as I did. The potential of a child's love can grow stronger in numbers, and we are stronger when we go against the odds together. I'm fighting to leave footprints for babies born into the same tragedy as me. There is a path you can follow that leads to your dreams, but it only exist if you remain consistent in making a difference. If you fail to remain consistent, you'll encounter more wilderness to cut through; because you didn't stay focused when the trail was clear. A change is going to come, because we're the future that'll carry on what our parents started. We're the water that'll quench our family trees thirst; both new twigs and old branches. I'm strong enough to fight every battle, I'm wise enough to make the right decision; and I'm mature enough to purchase the blessings You have in store for me.

I'm writing You this letter because I wanted to say thank You. Thank You for receiving my mail, guiding my footsteps, and being a number one DAD when my physical father was never there. Thank You for teaching me how to walk, and teaching me how to talk. Thank You for holding my brain in Your hands and guiding my mind in every thought. Thank You for being my force field when I walked through the field of serpents. Thank You for opening every letter I sent You, and reading my prayers from beginning to end. Thank You for blessing me with my talents. Everything I see in nature was once a design that sparked from an idea; just like the millions of ideas running around in my head. A vision without exertion is solely just a dream. You made Your dreams come true, and I too can rise and shine like the bright morning sun; like Father like son.

Not from Lance, but from the Heart of his Soul,

Your Child,

Lance

EPILOGUE

What daddy didn't know is that his boy upgraded and became a man. Although he was absent in my life, I had a Heavenly Father who nurtured my growth from a seed to adulthood; and He can do the same for you.

We must make responsible choices in life, or else one may end up dead or in prison not knowing their offspring. Regardless of how bad our circumstances in life are, we must not let it determine our future and our desire to succeed.

Parents must make a real effort to connect and mentor their children through spiritual guidance and conversations regarding the real world. It's important for parents to strive, reach out their helping hands, and mentor the youth in their community; because you never know how much of a difference you could impact on someone's life.

If you're a fatherless child, or even a motherless child, always remember that you're never alone. When you're feeling melancholy, and it seems like no one is there for you; remember that you have a Heavenly Father to pray to, and He'll never leave you by your lonesome. He'll help you climb every mountain, and hurdle every obstacle that life throws at you.

I say thank you to the fathers around the world who are making a difference, and for the fathers who aren't, I'm telling you to grow a pair and play your role. Be a man; nurture the seed you planted, and never leave it unattended. Don't be a contributor to the crisis of the fatherless tragedy.

Contact the Author

facebook.com/lancebrazelton

twitter.com/lancebrazelton

lancebrazelton.com

Booking Information

For booking or more information,

Contact Lance at
brazelton100@gmail.com

Acknowledgments

Kenny Anderson

Clifton Baker

Stephanie Baker

Trent Bennett

Victor Blade

Tyrus Brackett

Mozell Brazelton

Natalie Brazelton

Vickie Brazelton

Marcia Burnette

Cassandra Burruss

Mary Burns

Anita Cross

Larry Cunningham

Tyler Davis

David Denson

Joetta Di Bella

Calvin Drake

Robert Drake

Debbie Dryer

Gilbert Edwards

Sadler Evans

Richard Fletcher

Kenneth Goggans

Walter Griffin

Byron Hammons

Michael Hampton

Tammy Hampton

Jeff Hardin

Kelvin Hardin

Orenthia Henlon

Steven Jackson

Raleigh Johnson

Dexter Kennedy

Vernon Knight

Victoria Knight

Brenda Darcel
Harris-Lee

Yusuf Jamal Lee

Johnny Little

Doug Martinson

Mario Maitland

Christina McBeth

Shaun Miller

Barnard Nealy

Hayword Owens

Maurice Porter

Randel Richmond

Michelle Sisson

Richard Surles

Dalton Thompson

Carol Tucker

Nero Tucker

Pastor Jermaine
Turner

John Washington

Othel Washington

Kenny Watts

Kevin Wieseman

Carol Williamson

Norman Woody

Anatony Woods

Carlos Woods

60723215R10108

Made in the USA
Lexington, KY
16 February 2017